The NO (self) DOUBT Workbook

125 Exercises to Ditch Your Inner Critic and Increase Your Self-Confidence

MOLLY BURFORD
Author of *The No Worries Workbook* and *Stop Overthinking*

ADAMS MEDIA
New York Amsterdam/Antwerp London Toronto Sydney/Melbourne New Delhi

Adamsmedia
Adams Media
An Imprint of Simon & Schuster, LLC
100 Technology Center Drive
Stoughton, MA 02072

For more than 100 years, Simon & Schuster has championed authors and the stories they create. By respecting the copyright of an author's intellectual property, you enable Simon & Schuster and the author to continue publishing exceptional books for years to come. We thank you for supporting the author's copyright by purchasing an authorized edition of this book.

No amount of this book may be reproduced or stored in any format, nor may it be uploaded to any website, database, language-learning model, or other repository, retrieval, or artificial intelligence system without express permission. All rights reserved. Inquiries may be directed to Simon & Schuster, 1230 Avenue of the Americas, New York, NY 10020 or permissions@simonandschuster.com.

Copyright © 2026 by Simon & Schuster, LLC.

All rights reserved, including the right to reproduce this book or portions thereof in any form whatsoever. For information, address Adams Media Subsidiary Rights Department, 1230 Avenue of the Americas, New York, NY 10020.

First Adams Media trade paperback edition March 2026

ADAMS MEDIA and colophon are registered trademarks of Simon & Schuster, LLC.

Simon & Schuster strongly believes in freedom of expression and stands against censorship in all its forms. For more information, visit BooksBelong.com.

For information about special discounts for bulk purchases, please contact Simon & Schuster Special Sales at 1-866-506-1949 or business@simonandschuster.com.

The Simon & Schuster Speakers Bureau can bring authors to your live event. For more information or to book an event, contact the Simon & Schuster Speakers Bureau at 1-866-248-3049 or visit our website at www.simonspeakers.com.

Interior design by Priscilla Yuen
Interior images © Adobe Stock;
Simon & Schuster, LLC

Manufactured in the United States of America

1 2026

ISBN 978-1-5072-2526-4

Many of the designations used by manufacturers and sellers to distinguish their products are claimed as trademarks. Where those designations appear in this book and Simon & Schuster, LLC, was aware of a trademark claim, the designations have been printed with initial capital letters.

This book is intended as general information only and should not be used to diagnose or treat any health condition. In light of the complex, individual, and specific nature of health problems, this book is not intended to replace professional medical advice. The ideas, procedures, and suggestions in this book are intended to supplement, not replace, the advice of a trained medical professional. Consult your physician before adopting any of the suggestions in this book, as well as about any condition that may require diagnosis or medical attention. The author and publisher disclaim any liability arising directly or indirectly from the use of this book.

CONTENTS

■ INTRODUCTION 6

■ THE BASICS OF SELF-DOUBT 8

What Is Self-Doubt?................. **9**

Why Is Self-Doubt So Harmful?..... **9**

What Are the Causes of
Self-Doubt?........................... **10**

What Are the Symptoms of
Self-Doubt?........................... **10**

How Do You Overcome
Self-Doubt?........................... **12**

■ ACTIVITIES 13

Write a Self-Compassionate
Letter for a Bad Day................. **14**

Show Up for Yourself in These
Ways **15**

Be a Self-Historian: Where Does
Your Self-Doubt Come From? **16**

Remember Your Strengths......... **18**

Acknowledge Your Weaknesses.... **19**

Replace Your Negative Self-Talk
with Positive Self-Talk............... **20**

Make a Self-Confidence Playlist.... **21**

Stop Fearing Success **22**

Notice Your Self-Doubt
Warning Signs **24**

Design Your Most Confident Life .. **26**

Check In with Yourself **28**

List Your Past Achievements........ **29**

Create a Self-Esteem
Morning Routine **30**

Recall a Major Triumph............. **31**

Interrogate Your
Self-Doubting Beliefs **32**

Observe Your Thoughts............. **34**

Remember What You Learned
from the Mistake **35**

Fire Your Inner Critic **36**

Figure Out an Alternate Route **38**

Try These Self-Forgiveness
Affirmations.......................... **40**

List Your Needs **41**

Invest In Your Future **42**

Remember a Time You
Felt Self-Confident **44**

Face Your Self-Doubt Directly **45**

Dream Bigger........................ **46**

Comfort Your Inner Child **47**

Ask for Help (Without Shame)...... **48**

Give Yourself a Break............... **49**

Find Evidence of Your Self-Worth... **50**

Be Honest with Yourself about
What Isn't Working.................. **52**

Quit Procrastinating **53**

- List Three Good Things That Happened Today 54
- Establish Unconditional Self-Worth 55
- Express Yourself with These Activities 56
- Finish These Self-Empowering Statements 57
- Celebrate Your Little Wins 58
- Practice Positive Self-Talk 60
- Protect Your Peace 61
- Create a Compliment Log 62
- Make a Small Decision Without Consulting Anyone 64
- List What You Like about Yourself ... 65
- Make a Promise to Yourself to Build Self-Trust 66
- Spend Time with People Who Fill You Up 67
- Set Up Your Day for Self-Love 68
- List What You Can Control 70
- List What You Can't Control 71
- Schedule In More Joy 72
- Don't Bite Off More Than You Can Chew 74
- Recite Self-Compassion Coping Statements 76
- Know Your Boundaries with Loved Ones 77
- Define Success on *Your* Terms 78
- Give Yourself Flowers 80
- Write a Comforting Letter to Your Inner Teen 81
- Learn to Accept a Compliment 82
- Reassure Yourself with These Affirmations 83
- Track Your Little Actions for Your Big Goals 84
- Try This Self-Acceptance Meditation 86
- Practice Gratitude 87
- Be Nonjudgmental about Your Experience 88
- Remember That It's about Progress, Not Perfection 89
- Text Your Future Self 90
- Reduce Your Stress with These Activities 92
- Stop Selling Yourself Short 93
- Draw What Happiness Looks Like to You 94
- Do the Hard Thing First 96
- Focus On What You *Really* Want ... 97
- Reconnect with Your Inner Voice ... 98
- Reframe the Failure 99
- Take a Breath 100
- Do One Thing for Your Future Self Today 101
- Plan a Self-Care Day 102
- List Your Needs 103
- Explore Your Values 104
- Embrace Your Imperfections 106
- Measure Your Worth Differently ... 107
- Remember That You Can't Do It All (And That's Okay) 108
- Do a Social Media Comparison Cleanse 109

Give Yourself More Credit 110	Be More Aware of Yourself 146
Build Yourself Up 112	Be Grateful for Your Shortcomings 147
Consider a Different Perspective ... 113	
Set Realistic Expectations 114	Challenge Your Negative Thoughts 148
Finish These Self-Awareness Statements 116	Be Your Own Best Friend 149
Say These Self-Worth Affirmations 117	Chase Your Dreams 150
	Try Something Again 151
Be Mindful of Your Self-Doubt Catchphrases 118	Acknowledge How Far You've Come 152
Embrace That You're Not Everyone's Cup of Tea 119	Develop a Growth Mindset 154
Fail Forward 120	Draw a Vision Board of Your Hopes 155
Draw a Self-Portrait 122	Stop Judging Yourself 156
Improve Your Self-Image 123	Repeat These Self-Acceptance Affirmations 158
Understand Impostor Syndrome ... 124	
Track Your Progress 126	Validate Your Feelings 159
Ask Your Younger Self for Advice ... 128	Cut Yourself Some Slack 160
Don't Overcommit 129	Create a Self-Esteem Night Routine 162
Try Loving-Kindness Meditation .. 130	
Practice Self-Forgiveness 132	Choose Yourself 163
Do Something for Someone Else .. 134	Draw Your Most Confident Self ... 164
Set Five Small Goals to Accomplish This Week 135	Be the Hero of Your Own Story ... 165
Consider the Source 136	Practice Assertive Communication 166
List Three Good Decisions You've Made in the Past 137	Get Organized with These Tasks .. 168
	Reroute Self-Critical Thoughts 170
Make an Action Plan 138	Plan Your Daily Nonnegotiables for Self-Care 172
Build Self-Esteem with These Activities 140	
Create a Self-Compassion Log ... 142	Take a Self-Compassion Break 173
Quit Comparing Yourself 143	
Find More Balance 144	■ **APPENDIX 174**

INTRODUCTION

Have you ever found yourself unable to make a decision because you aren't sure you'll make the "right" choice? Do you feel like an impostor, wondering when others will figure out that you don't know what you're doing? Or maybe you get so tied up in wanting things to be perfect that you feel frozen at the starting line. While everyone experiences self-doubt from time to time, it can end up taking over, impacting your day-to-day and preventing you from living your best life. From making you think every success you've ever had is a fluke to causing you to worry that you'll never be good enough, self-doubt is a convincing liar.

It's time to embrace the truth with *The No (Self) Doubt Workbook*! This book is filled with 125 creative, easy-to-follow activities to help you stop self-doubt in its tracks so you'll feel confident in yourself and your life. With activities ranging from fill-in-the-blanks, mindful meditations, and checklists, to journaling, planning, and drawing, you will:

You can work through these activities in order—or jump to the ones that stand out to you or that feel most helpful in the moment. It's all about what works best for *you* and *your* journey.

But before diving in, be sure to read through The Basics of Self-Doubt section on the following pages. There you'll learn more about self-doubt, including common symptoms—and how building self-confidence through the activities in this workbook can help you redirect negative self-talk to manifest more certainty in yourself and your decisions.

As you work through these activities, remember that self-doubt happens to the best of us. When you're used to beating yourself up and doubting every little thing you say or do, it's going to take time to rewire those impulses. But with some practice, you can leave self-doubt behind and take control of your future. So let's get to it!

The BASICS of SELF-DOUBT

Overcoming self-doubt starts with a better understanding of this debilitating frame of mind. Once you know what it actually is and how it shows up, self-doubt will be easier to recognize—and overcome! In the following pages, you'll learn the basics of self-doubt, including signs to look for, and how to build self-confidence in place of the doubt. With these basics in mind, you'll be better equipped to move through this workbook and make the most of each activity.

WHAT IS SELF-DOUBT?

In simple terms, self-doubt is a lack of confidence in yourself and your abilities. When you feel unsure about what you can achieve and your overall worth, you're doubting yourself. While everyone questions themselves once in a while, persistent self-doubt goes beyond this. Some common examples of self-doubt include:

- *A nagging feeling that you aren't good at anything*
- *Believing you don't matter very much*
- *Not challenging yourself because you don't see the point in trying*
- *Never going after your big dreams because you don't think you can achieve them*

You may notice more than one of these experiences happening at the same time, or it may feel like life is emphasizing a particular doubt you have about yourself. Either way, it's an uncomfortable feeling, and one that, as you'll read about in the next section, can get in the way of your well-being.

WHY IS SELF-DOUBT SO HARMFUL?

Self-doubt can have a huge impact on your overall sense of self. It can make you feel worthless and exhausted. These feelings of worthlessness reinforce self-doubt, compounding your negative beliefs about yourself and making them stronger. It can also act as a self-fulfilling prophecy in a way, leading you to quit something before you even give yourself the chance to truly try and put in the effort. You might think "Why bother?" when presented with an opportunity or challenge because you're convinced you'll fail anyway.

Self-doubt can negatively impact your life in many ways, all of which ultimately keep you from living up to your fullest potential. You may avoid professional or personal opportunities that can be invaluable for growth and wellness. Your relationships with others may be limited by your feelings of insecurity, which make it difficult to communicate your thoughts and feelings. Additionally, self-doubt can trigger chronic indecisiveness, even in small matters, and anxiety, where your mind seems to constantly be clouded with intrusive, fearful thoughts.

WHAT ARE THE CAUSES OF SELF-DOUBT?

A lot of things can spark self-doubt. These experiences can build on each other, causing you to continually doubt yourself. Some factors that often underlie self-doubt include:

- **Childhood experiences** *Adverse events during childhood can lead you to develop self-doubt. Bullying, criticism, trauma, or a lack of support can leave you vulnerable.*
- **Past failures** *Mistakes or failures in your past may make you afraid to try things again.*
- **Negative self-talk** *Consistently criticizing yourself can lead to a deeper sense of self-doubt.*
- **Impostor syndrome** *The belief that you are a "fraud" can make you doubt yourself and your own abilities.*

Again, overarching self-doubt can stem from a number of these factors, and can also manifest in different ways—as you'll discover in the next section.

WHAT ARE THE SYMPTOMS OF SELF-DOUBT?

Self-doubt might be keeping you from living your best life. Its symptoms are easy to identify. The following are telltale signs that your life may be affected by self-doubt:

Anxiety   Feeling fearful and anxious is a hallmark of self-doubt. You might always think you're forgetting something or doing something wrong.

Depression   Self-doubt often pairs with depression. You might struggle with an overall feeling of hopelessness or pointlessness.

Lack of motivation   Self-doubt can make you feel unmotivated, stopping you from going after the things you want out of life.

Shame and guilt   These twin emotions are often triggered by self-doubt, leading you to believe that you're worthless, inherently bad, or have done something wrong.

Procrastination   Fear of failure spurred by self-doubt can cause you to constantly put things off.

Reassurance-seeking   Self-doubt can lead you to constantly seek external validation from other people to compensate for a lack of belief in yourself.

Self-deprecating jokes   Self-doubt can show up as this type of humor. Putting yourself down in a joking way is often a sign of low self-esteem.

Freeze response   Self-doubt can cause a freeze response when you're faced with a challenge, where you literally feel like you can't move to complete the challenge.

Negative self-talk   Self-doubt can show up as speaking to and about yourself unkindly.

Avoidance of challenges   Your internal self-doubting voice can tell you that you'll fail anyway, so why bother even trying?

Lack of boundaries   Self-doubt may be a factor if you have trouble setting boundaries. When you feel bad about yourself, you may seek the approval of others, even if that results in detrimental outcomes.

Comparison *Self-doubt can encourage you to compare yourself to others. You might find yourself constantly scanning your social media feeds, comparing your life to the highlight reels of others, looking for evidence that you are as worthless as you feel.*

Perfectionism *Self-doubt can make you become a perfectionist, meaning you're never fully satisfied with your success unless you feel it's "perfect." (And nothing is ever perfect in life.)*

When self-doubt creeps in, it can take over your life. Luckily, the right tools, mindset, and strategies can help you overcome it!

HOW DO YOU OVERCOME SELF-DOUBT?

Self-doubt can be faced head-on *and* defeated by building self-confidence. Self-confidence is that internal belief in yourself, your worth, and your abilities. It's the willingness to take charge of your own life and the faith that you will figure things out, even if they don't go the way you initially thought they would.

So how do you build self-confidence? The activities in this workbook will help; they are designed with this goal in mind. Each practice targets that underlying lack of confidence with tried-and-true strategies like engaging in positive self-talk, prioritizing self-care, finding the lessons in difficult situations, celebrating your triumphs, forgiving yourself for past mistakes, and more.

With a bit of effort and a willingness to tolerate some discomfort, you can claim your power and start believing in yourself. Because here's the thing: You are good at many things, and you do matter! You matter a lot, actually. And you are so much more powerful than you realize. You deserve to feel good about yourself and to go after the life you want. So without further ado, it's time to say goodbye to self-doubt!

ACTIVITIES

Write a Self-Compassionate Letter for a Bad Day

Unfortunately, you're going to have bad days in this life. They come with the territory of being human. Whether it involves a mistake at work or a fight with your best friend, you're going to have moments that make you feel small and defeated.

And on those bad days, self-compassion is what's going to get you through the pain.

WHAT TO DO

Here you're going to write yourself a self-compassionate letter for bad days. You can wait to write the letter in response to a specific scenario, or you're welcome to compose an all-purpose self-compassionate letter. Whatever works best for you!

Show Up for Yourself in These Ways

Knowing how to show up for yourself can be difficult when you're full of self-doubt. If you're preoccupied with insecurities and feelings of low self-worth, it makes sense you'd forget what you need to do to take care of yourself and be your own best friend.

Luckily, this exercise is here to help with a list of simple ways to put your well-being front and center.

WHAT TO DO

Use this self-care checklist to track your progress as you practice providing yourself the care you deserve:

- [ ] *Call a trusted friend to vent.*
- [ ] *Say no when you need to.*
- [ ] *Ask for help. (See the Ask for Help (Without Shame) activity for tips.)*
- [ ] *Take a long, hot shower.*
- [ ] *Journal.*
- [ ] *Do a meditation exercise.*
- [ ] *Go for a walk.*
- [ ] *Listen to your self-confidence playlist! (See Make a Self-Confidence Playlist.)*
- [ ] *Silence your phone and focus on what you need to get done.*

Be a Self-Historian: Where Does Your Self-Doubt Come From?

Everything has a history, including your self-doubt. From singular core memories to cyclical events, your self-doubt has been built and reinforced over time.

Understanding the roots of your self-doubt gives you the chance to both identify and challenge negative thought patterns and behaviors. In so doing, you're able to face your self-doubt directly and therefore break it down.

WHAT TO DO

In this exercise, you'll act as a self-historian, creating a timeline of your self-doubt. List key events in your self-doubt history. Write down all pertinent information you remember about each situation, including your age, what happened, and how it made you feel.

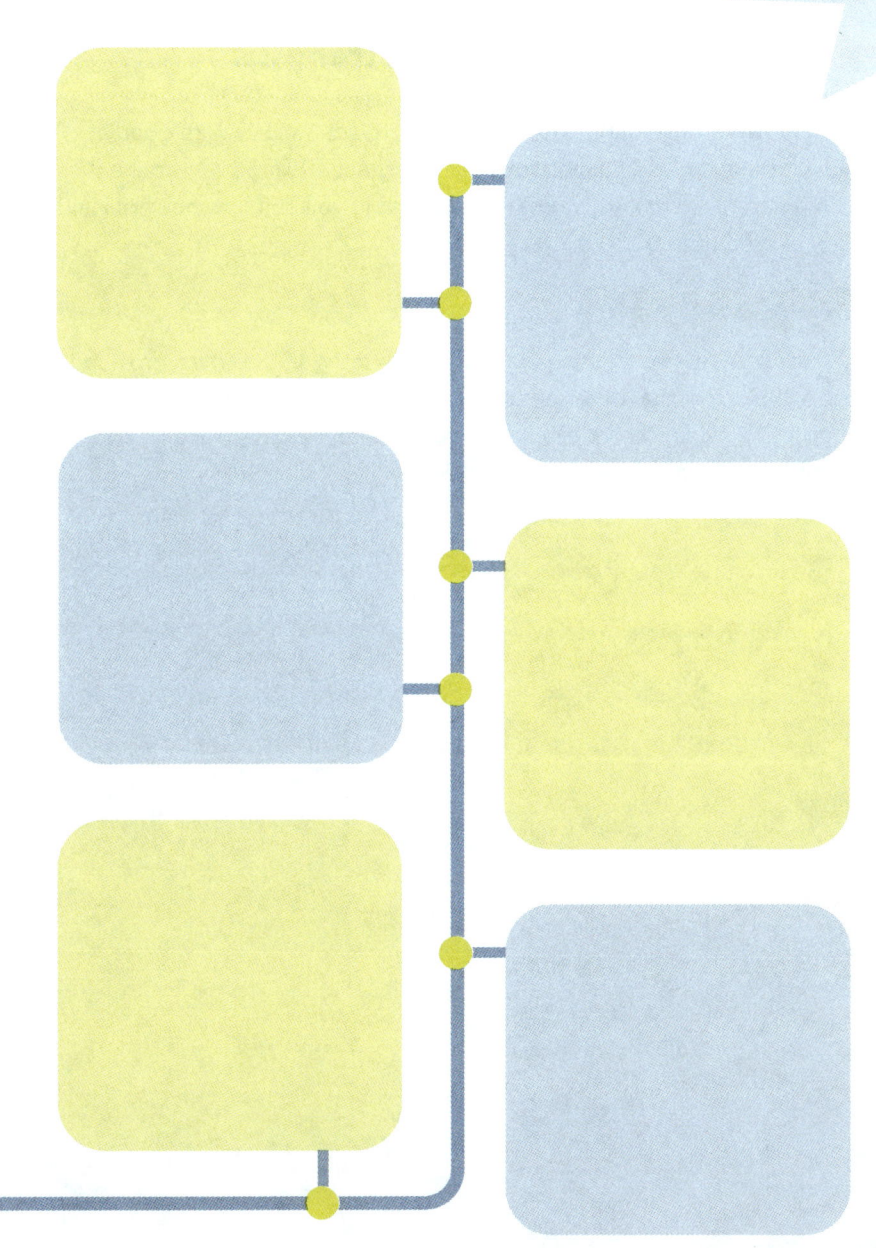

Remember Your Strengths

Despite what self-doubt might tell you, there are things you're good at. In fact, there are even things you're totally great at! That's why you're going to remember your strengths—to remind yourself how powerful and capable you truly are.

WHAT TO DO

In this exercise, you're going to list your strengths. In the space provided, use an adjective that describes a strength you have, and then provide supporting evidence. For example: "I am patient. I always make time to listen to my friends when they're struggling."

Acknowledge Your Weaknesses

You're human, which means you're not perfect. You have flaws, and that's totally okay. If anything, your imperfections make you a more interesting person! Perfection is boring.

Owning your flaws is an essential component of self-awareness and, therefore, self-confidence. By knowing where you could improve and what your limitations are, you'll become more self-assured because you'll understand yourself better.

WHAT TO DO

List some of your flaws. Then write out how you can either (A) improve or (B) accept the limitation. For example: "I'm not great at math. That's why they invented calculators!"

Flaw: _____.
How I can improve or accept it: _____
_____.

Flaw: _____.
How I can improve or accept it: _____
_____.

Flaw: _____.
How I can improve or accept it: _____
_____.

Flaw: _____.
How I can improve or accept it: _____
_____.

Flaw: _____.
How I can improve or accept it: _____
_____.

Replace Your Negative Self-Talk with Positive Self-Talk

Negative self-talk happens to the best of us, but you can break the cycle of negativity with effort, self-awareness, and, yes, a smidge of discomfort. All it takes is a little positive back talk.

WHAT TO DO

In the space provided, write down a recurring negative self-talk thought. For example: "I'm never good enough." Then add a positive self-talk statement that challenges that notion and turns the self-doubt around. For example: "I *am* good enough, even if I don't feel like it sometimes. My worth is not dependent on my productivity."

Make a Self-Confidence Playlist

Music can have a major influence on your emotions and mood. Finding songs that make you feel empowered, capable, and happy can help you tune out self-doubt and jam along to the rhythm of confidence.

WHAT TO DO

Start brainstorming songs that make you feel like your best self. List the song titles on the lines provided and then make your own playlist on your favorite streaming service.

-
-
-
-
-
-
-
-
-
-
-
-
-
-
-

Stop Fearing Success

When you fear success, sometimes it's because you feel like you don't have what it takes to keep up with its demands. Other times, it might be because you're unsure of what that success might bring, and that uncertainty makes you squirm.

Ultimately, though, a fear of success is driven by self-doubt—a lack of confidence in your ability to hold on to success once you have it. This exercise is going to help you conquer those fears and embrace the success you deserve.

WHAT TO DO

Write down all the reasons you can think of to fear being successful. For example, maybe you're terrified of looking "cringe," or perhaps you're convinced that eventually success will transform into failure.

Once you've come up with your list of reasons, reframe those fears by writing down self-empowering statements. For example: "People can think I'm cringe because I'd rather do what I love than be trapped in a life that isn't my own."

My **FEARS**

_____
_____
_____
_____
_____
_____
_____

SELF-EMPOWERING *Statements*

Notice Your Self-Doubt Warning Signs

Sometimes that debilitating, self-doubting inner voice can be whispering its nonsense in your ear for hours without you even noticing, working to convince you that you aren't worthy of the things you want or have. This exercise will help you learn to recognize your self-doubt warning signs so you'll be better equipped to quiet the self-doubting chatter and respond to life with self-confidence instead.

WHAT TO DO

List some of your self-doubt warning signs. For each, include specific examples that illustrate how it leads to self-doubt for you. For example, having trouble accepting compliments is a prime example of a self-doubt warning sign.

Design Your Most Confident Life

Finding the most confident version of yourself sometimes takes a little effort. The activities in this exercise create a framework with which to work on your self-confidence. And self-confidence is a surefire antidote to self-doubt.

WHAT TO DO

Use the following chart and to-do list to design your most confident life. Each prompt is meant to remind you about what you're good at and how you can incorporate more of those strengths into your day-to-day life, boosting your self-esteem. Once you've filled in the chart, create a daily to-do list for using your strengths and building your confidence.

What I Love Doing	What I'm Good At	What I Can Work On	How I Can Improve	Daily Self-Love To-Do List

What I Love Doing	What I'm Good At	What I Can Work On	How I Can Improve	Daily Self-Love To-Do List

My DAILY CONFIDENCE-BOOSTING To-Dos:

- _____
- _____
- _____
- _____
- _____
- _____
- _____
- _____

Check In with Yourself

Part of conquering self-doubt involves understanding yourself. After all, the more you know yourself, the more confident you'll feel because you'll know you've got your own back. You'll accept your limitations, acknowledge your strengths, and navigate your life with more self-assuredness. You'll also realize when your self-doubt is taking over and steering you away from reality. Here you're going to check in with yourself emotionally when you're feeling extra doubtful of your worth.

WHAT TO DO

Use this chart to write down everything you're feeling regarding your emotions right now. Include specific emotions, where you feel each one in your body, and anything else that feels relevant to your current emotional state.

EMOTION	PHYSICAL FEELING	NOTES

Now take a few deep breaths and read what you wrote. Hopefully you'll be able to see which specific emotions may be clouding your judgment, allowing you to recognize the self-doubt for exactly what it is.

List Your Past Achievements

You've accomplished more than you think you have. You're doing so much better than you allow yourself to believe. Having trouble believing that? Okay, no problem. You're going to remind yourself now of just how much you have conquered.

WHAT TO DO

On the following lines, list some of your past achievements. They could be big, small, or anywhere in between.

-
-
-
-
-
-
-
-
-
-
-
-
-
-
-

Create a Self-Esteem Morning Routine

You can begin to set up your day for high self-esteem as soon as you wake up in the morning! Creating a morning routine that focuses on confidence and happiness is a great way to curb self-doubt.

WHAT TO DO

Feel good about yourself first thing in the morning by scheduling some tasks that will boost your self-esteem. Setting a specific time (the earlier the better!) will make it more likely you'll keep to the schedule. For example: "I will start my day at 7 a.m. and do a self-love affirmation."

TIME:	TASK:

Recall a Major Triumph

In case you've forgotten, you have done some pretty wonderful things in your life. Some major things, in fact. This exercise will remind you of those wins.

WHAT TO DO

Draw a big win that made you feel empowered and proud of yourself. This could be landing a job you *really* wanted, winning an art contest, getting a good grade on a super hard test . . . whatever comes to mind! The point is that it felt major to *you*.

Interrogate Your Self-Doubting Beliefs

No matter how convincing it may seem, your self-doubt is lying to you. That inner voice might say you aren't capable, that your accomplishments are a fluke, or that you're worthless, but these are all lies. It's up to you to uncover the truth. And that's exactly what you're going to do here!

WHAT TO DO

Here, you will interrogate your self-doubt. In each beam of light, write down the lie your self-doubt is telling you (e.g., "You don't deserve a promotion; why even apply?"). Then give the reasons why that statement is not valid (e.g., "You work hard; you meet deadlines; you are a team player. You should apply for the promotion.").

Observe Your Thoughts

Mindfulness helps combat self-doubt because it allows you to take a step out of your head and into the present moment. Self-doubt is often future-based, and mindfulness can be a useful strategy for bringing yourself back to the here and now.

There are many ways to practice mindfulness; this exercise provides one technique that's especially helpful if you struggle with self-doubt.

WHAT TO DO

Here you're simply going to observe your thoughts. Find a quiet, calm area and sit in a comfortable position. Close your eyes and take a few deep breaths. Then allow thoughts to slowly float into your mind. For each thought, just observe it, kind of like how you'd look at a leaf falling from a tree. Detach yourself from that thought and just watch it fall away. This will help you calm your mind, and a calm mind is better able to conquer self-doubt.

Remember What You Learned from the Mistake

A fact: You will make mistakes; it's part of being alive and being human. You're going to say the awkward thing in a group chat; you're going to be late for work; you're going to annoy your mom. You're not perfect, and that's okay. Just remember that everything is a learning opportunity.

WHAT TO DO

This exercise will help you find the lesson learned in a mistake that you're still beating yourself up over. In the space provided, journal about the mistake and then reflect on the lesson. For example: "Ugh, I was so late for work today. Next time, I'll get up ten minutes earlier to mitigate the fallout of any unexpected traffic."

Fire Your Inner Critic

Your inner critic has been working hard, but not smart. It's been chirping in your ear, filling your mind with doubts and worries, impacting your focus and self-esteem. Well, enough is enough. It's time to take charge and fire your inner critic.

WHAT TO DO

In this activity, you're going to fire your inner critic by writing a termination letter in which you outline its poor performance. On the following page, write a letter to your inner critic as if it's an employee. List all the reasons why you're letting them go and why they aren't a good fit for your life anymore.

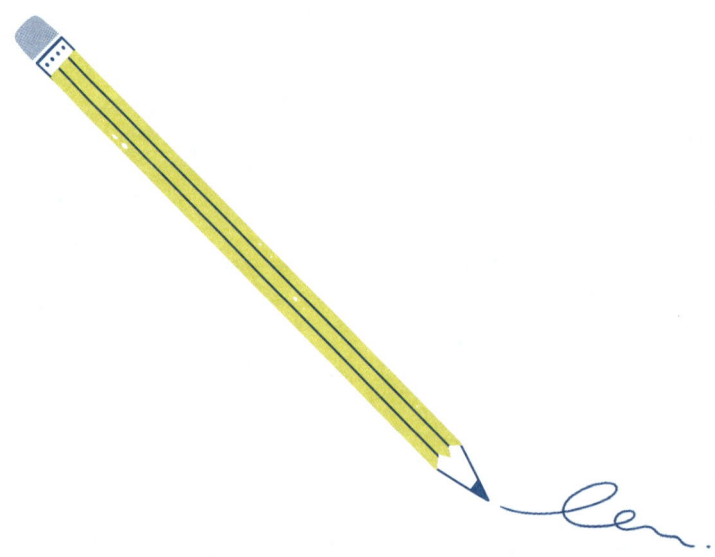

Figure Out an Alternate Route

Let's face it: Things don't always go according to plan. It's just part of life, but that's half the fun of the journey, right? What a pleasure it can be to take new routes and gain fresh perspectives! After all, you can learn a lot about yourself and your strengths when you have to reroute.

Finding innovative ways to deal with unforeseen circumstances can help you build self-confidence and banish self-doubt because it serves as proof that you're capable of handling whatever life throws your way.

WHAT TO DO

This activity gives you an opportunity to practice figuring out alternate routes. In each road detour sign on the next page, write down next step(s) you can take to get around the obstacle. For example, let's say you had to stay late at the office, meaning you had to miss a scheduled workout class. Instead of skipping exercise altogether that day, you could simply go for a walk with your dog instead. Or, you could take the night off and sign up for a new class the following day. This will help you learn to trust your instincts and problem solve, both of which are imperative for defeating self-doubt.

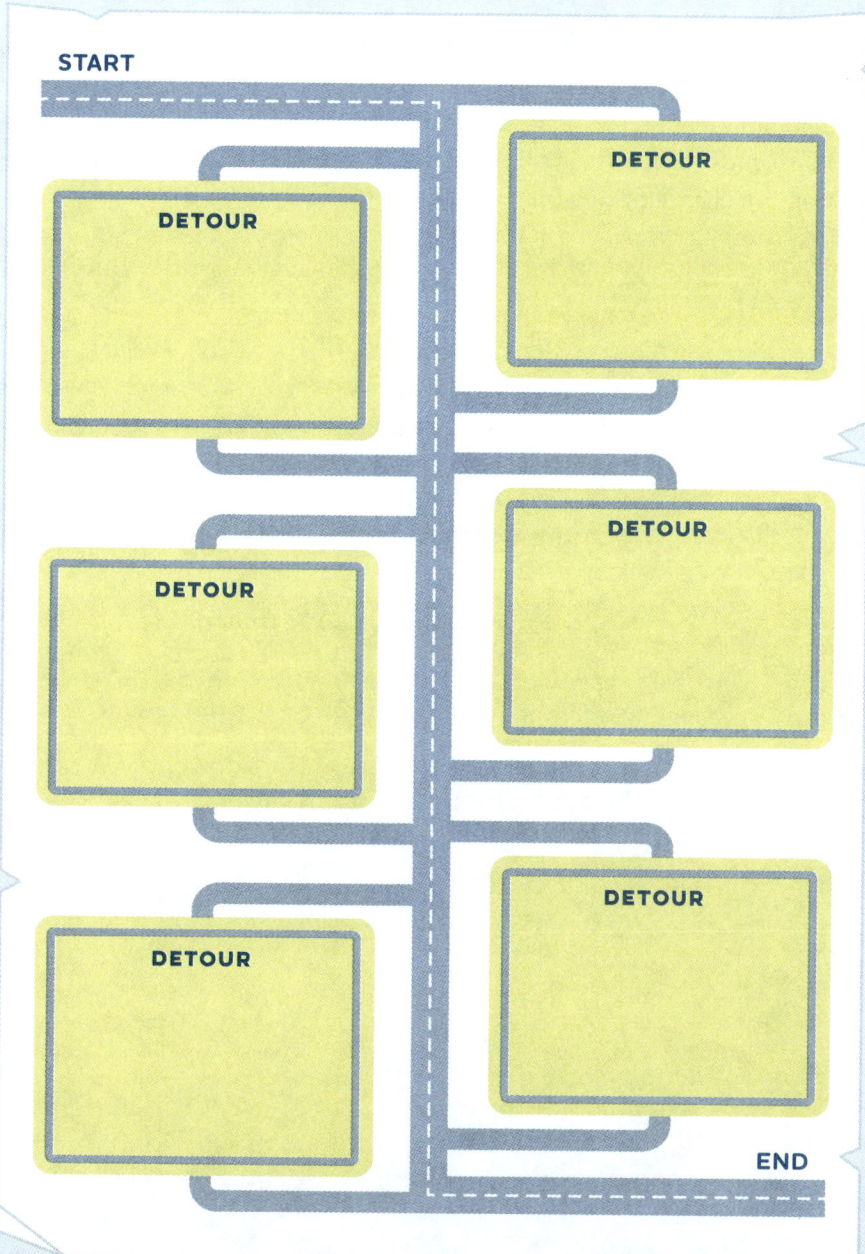

Try These Self-Forgiveness Affirmations

Self-forgiveness is one of the first steps toward self-love. More self-forgiveness can lead to improved mental and emotional well-being, as well as higher self-esteem and a lowered risk for anxiety and depression. These results will put you in a better place for conquering self-doubt.

WHAT TO DO

Recite some of these self-forgiveness statements out loud. Highlight any that are particularly helpful or resonate with you, and return to these whenever negative feelings strike. There are also a few blank lines where you can write your own self-forgiveness affirmations!

Everyone makes mistakes, including me.

I will learn something valuable from this.

Nobody is perfect.   *I can grow from this.*

I forgive myself for this shortcoming.

List Your Needs

Everyone has unique needs, and the better you understand your own needs, the better you'll be able to care for yourself. Good self-knowledge and good self-care equal good self-esteem.

WHAT TO DO

List your major needs along with action steps for making sure you meet them every single day. For example: "I need to take care of my physical needs daily. I can do this through healthy eating, hygiene, exercise, and proper sleep."

-
-
-
-
-
-
-
-

Invest In Your Future

Self-doubt has a way of creeping in when you're worrying about the future. Maybe you have to make a presentation at work and you're filled with dread that you won't be sufficiently prepared and will botch it. Whatever the upcoming scenario you may be stressing over, there are plenty of things you can do to set yourself up for success. Sometimes it's all about how you look at things. This exercise will help you reframe your outlook so you can ensure the win!

WHAT TO DO

You can only do the best you can with the time you have. Fill in the following prompts to help you plan accordingly for whatever event you're worried about. A sense of preparedness will give you more self-assurance and the confidence to realize you can handle this.

What I'm worried about:

_____
_____
_____
_____

Why I'm worried:

_____
_____
_____
_____

How I can reframe this worry:

_____
_____
_____
_____

How I can prepare:

_____
_____
_____
_____
_____

How it went:

_____
_____
_____
_____
_____
_____

Remember a Time You Felt Self-Confident

When self-doubt is swirling in your mind, it can be easy to forget that you've had moments of self-confidence in your life. There were times when you handled a situation with self-assuredness, taking charge with clarity and grace. Remembering these moments can help launch you back into that confident mindset now.

WHAT TO DO

Journal about a time you felt totally confident and capable. Include what was going on, who you were with, how you felt, and what helped you navigate everything with such confidence. Be as specific as possible:

Face Your Self-Doubt Directly

Sometimes you don't realize how pervasive an insecurity actually is. With a million thoughts swirling through your head daily, you can't focus on each one. However, that doesn't mean your thoughts don't make an impact! Your subconscious mind is powerful and constantly percolating.

WHAT TO DO

In this exercise, you'll face those underlying self-doubts directly by getting them out in the open. Write down everything you feel insecure about, from your career to your love life to your appearance—anything you struggle with. Looking at your self-doubts head-on will help you learn to love and accept the challenges they may present.

Dream Bigger

Sometimes self-doubt causes you to aim way smaller than you should. When you doubt yourself, you're bound to fail because of your mistaken belief that you won't be able to achieve the things you want. However, this just isn't true. You're capable of meeting big challenges, and you deserve to shoot for the stars.

WHAT TO DO

On this page, draw your wildest dreams for your future self. They could be related to your dream career, your dream relationship, your dream house—any of life's major occasions. Don't be afraid to dream big.

Comfort Your Inner Child

Even though you're an adult, a part of your childhood self still exists within you. You might not realize it, but this inner child plays a huge role in your life. In fact, many of your self-doubting beliefs were probably formed in childhood. It's time to comfort your inner child to help ease those doubts.

WHAT TO DO

Go back in time to meet your inner child during a difficult situation from childhood. For example, let's say your dad spoke to you unkindly in a moment of anger and you still hear his critical voice. Envision the scene, and imagine yourself entering the room as an adult. Hug your childhood self and tell your dad that *he* has the problem, and that you deserve love and compassion. You can use the space provided to reflect on the situation and how you comfort your inner child.

Ask for Help (Without Shame)

No one gets through this life alone. We all need help every now and then, and there's nothing wrong with that. Knowing when to ask (and how to ask) will ensure you get the assistance you need, when you need it.

WHAT TO DO

In this exercise, you're going to answer a series of questions that will help you prepare to ask someone for help with confidence. Fill in the following prompts to plan your conversation:

What do I need help with? _____

Is there a timeline? If so, what is it? _____

Who can I ask for help? _____

What could I say when asking? _____

How I felt after asking for help: _____

Give Yourself a Break

You deserve to give yourself a break every now and then. De-stressing is crucial for building self-worth and kicking self-doubt to the curb.

WHAT TO DO

Draw a relaxing scene of yourself taking a break. You could be on the beach, at a spa, or simply taking a nap. Visualizing this will help you take a step out of panic mode and into a calm place.

Find Evidence of Your Self-Worth

You are inherently worthy, even if you don't see that right now. That's why you're going to find all the evidence of your self-worth that exists!

WHAT TO DO

In each magnifying glass, write down something that proves your self-worth. For example: "I have self-worth because I exist" or "I have self-worth because I matter to my family."

Be Honest with Yourself about What Isn't Working

Part of dismantling self-doubt and leaning into self-confidence is learning how to trust yourself. And because self-trust is based on self-honesty, sometimes this means telling yourself truths you might not exactly want to hear. Don't worry, though; it's for the best!

WHAT TO DO

Being honest with yourself doesn't mean you have to be unkind to yourself in the process, especially when it's a difficult truth you must face. Here you'll work through the difficulties in a compassionate way.

Write down something in your life that isn't working. This could be your job, a friendship, or even how you spend your free time. Once you determine what it is that's not serving you well, get specific about why it's not aligned with the kind of life you want to live. From there, write down a self-affirming statement of how you're going to take your power back from the situation. Remember to give yourself grace as you reflect.

Quit Procrastinating

Procrastination: We've all been there. And sometimes procrastination is a symptom of self-doubt because it can be a form of avoidance when you don't think you're properly equipped to achieve something.

WHAT TO DO

Here you're going to begin work on a project you've been putting off. You'll prove yourself wrong: You are capable of doing it! This could be an assignment for school, a presentation for work, or any task at all really, even something as mundane as cleaning your bedroom. Remember, done is better than perfect.

In each bullet point, fill in the prompts to help you realize that procrastination is not protecting you; it's only making you suffer.

- *The task I'm procrastinating about:* _____

- *Why I'm avoiding the task:* _____

- *Date I am starting the task:* _____

- *How I felt after completing the task:* _____

List Three Good Things That Happened Today

Mindset is everything, and even on your most gray days, there are still silver linings to be found. This isn't to ignore your pain, but rather to put things in perspective and remember there are better days ahead, and good things to be found in today.

WHAT TO DO

In this activity, you're going to think of three good things that happened today in order to practice gratitude, lift yourself up, and get yourself into a positive mindset. List positive events both big and small; they all matter! For example, simply getting up at the first sound of your alarm without hitting the snooze button is a good thing.

Establish Unconditional Self-Worth

Unconditional self-worth is the belief that you have value no matter what. This means that you love yourself regardless of your accomplishments, productivity, social standing, relationship status, job, income, or anything else.

Unconditional self-worth is important for building self-esteem and saying goodbye to self-doubt; with unconditional self-worth, external validation matters less than your own relationship with yourself.

WHAT TO DO

In this exercise, you're going to practice unconditional self-worth by establishing benchmarks. Fill in the blanks with external conditions that might at times challenge your sense of self-worth. For example: "I still matter, even if I don't meet my income goal this year."

I still matter, even if _____.

I still matter, even if _____.

I still matter, even if _____.

I still matter, even if _____.

I still matter, even if _____.

I still matter, even if _____.

I still matter, even if _____.

I still matter, even if _____.

Express Yourself with These Activities

Self-expression is a great way to get to know yourself better, build self-trust, and enhance your sense of self. There are so many fun and creative ways you can express everything you are, from drawing to music to dance!

WHAT TO DO

The following is a list of suggested activities that can help you express yourself. Check off each one after you try it. Highlight activities you especially love.

- *Draw a self-portrait. (See the Draw a Self-Portrait exercise in this workbook.)*
- *Make a soundtrack playlist for a movie about your life.*
- *Write a poem about your favorite memory.*
- *Jot down a short story.*
- *Dance to your favorite music.*
- *Paint an abstract painting that illustrates your feelings with colors.*
- *Construct a collage.*
- *Make up a recipe.*
- *Create a junk journal.*
- *Journal about your day.*
- *Reflect on your past with a haiku.*
- *Rearrange the furniture in your home.*

Finish These Self-Empowering Statements

You deserve to feel empowered because you're more capable than you realize. You're strong and resilient and tough. You have conquered so much in your life and you will continue to be successful as the years go on.

WHAT TO DO

It's time to encourage yourself with self-empowering statements that quiet self-doubt and amplify self-confidence. For each fill-in-the-blank, finish the self-empowering statement to help you take charge of your life.

I can handle whatever comes my way because _____.

I am stronger than I realize because _____.

I can take charge because _____.

I am _____, which means I can do _____.

Celebrate Your Little Wins

Your little wins matter just as much as your major triumphs. Over time, even the smallest of successes accumulate to contribute to the development of greater self-confidence. You deserve to celebrate those small victories!

WHAT TO DO

Draw or write in each trophy about one of your little wins. It could be as simple as "I got out of bed on time today" or "I ate broccoli because I know how to nourish myself."

Practice Positive Self-Talk

Positive self-talk is a great method for building self-esteem and enhancing your sense of self. Positive self-talk involves speaking to yourself in an assuring, kind manner, especially during times of stress and self-doubt.

Positive self-talk can help reduce anxiety and stress, improve your self-image, and enhance resilience. It's always a good idea to speak to yourself lovingly.

WHAT TO DO

Here's a series of positive self-talk sentences. Say each sentence out loud while looking at yourself in a mirror. It might feel a little awkward or uncomfortable at first, especially if self-love is a new concept for you. That's okay! Keep pushing through; it gets easier with practice.

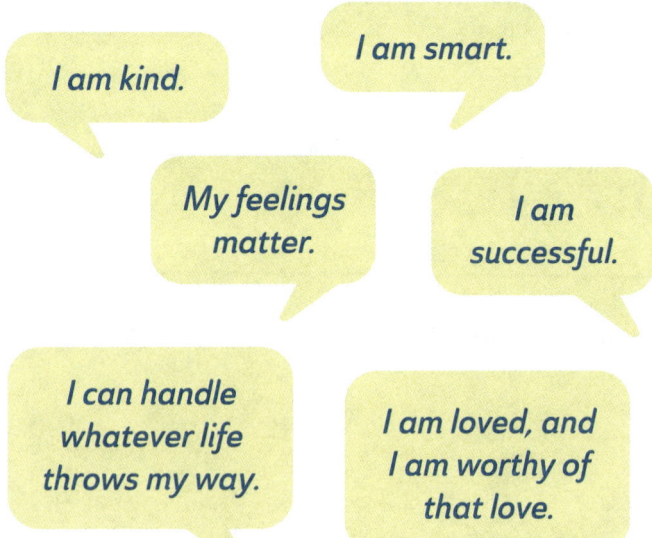

I am kind.

I am smart.

My feelings matter.

I am successful.

I can handle whatever life throws my way.

I am loved, and I am worthy of that love.

Protect Your Peace

Protecting your peace is vital for your well-being. Your serenity helps you see things from a calmer, sounder place, helping you navigate life with more confidence and grace.

WHAT TO DO

Here you're going to use mindfulness to protect your peace. This exercise is just one example of the many ways you can incorporate mindfulness into your life.

1. *Sit or lie down comfortably in a quiet, distraction-free place.*
2. *Take a few deep breaths.*
3. *As you continue to breathe, imagine the most peaceful scene you can think of. This could be your favorite place as a kid, the beach, or anywhere else that makes you feel safe and grounded.*
4. *As you visualize the peaceful place, imagine thunder clouds rolling in.*
5. *As each gray cloud comes into your mind's eye, imagine blowing it away from your peaceful area.*
6. *Repeat step 5 five times.*
7. *Slowly open your eyes. Take one more deep breath, and then move on with your day.*

Create a Compliment Log

Everyone loves getting compliments! It's nice to be affirmed. Compliments are especially helpful to remember when you're doubting yourself. That's why you're going to start a compliment log.

WHAT TO DO

Whenever you get a compliment from a friend, family member, coworker, or even a random stranger, make sure to log what they said and how it lifted your spirits. Then you can turn to this page whenever you're in need of a reminder about how amazing you truly are. Remembering your accolades will give your self-esteem a boost and help you conquer self-doubt.

NAME:	DATE: / /
COMPLIMENT:	HOW IT MADE ME FEEL:

NAME:	DATE: / /
COMPLIMENT:	HOW IT MADE ME FEEL:

NAME:	DATE: / /
COMPLIMENT:	HOW IT MADE ME FEEL:

NAME:	DATE: / /
COMPLIMENT:	HOW IT MADE ME FEEL:

NAME:	DATE: / /
COMPLIMENT:	HOW IT MADE ME FEEL:

NAME:	DATE: / /
COMPLIMENT:	HOW IT MADE ME FEEL:

NAME:	DATE: / /
COMPLIMENT:	HOW IT MADE ME FEEL:

Make a Small Decision Without Consulting Anyone

Self-doubt can cause you to distrust yourself. When you don't trust yourself, decision-making can be a struggle. The choice could be something as simple as what to eat for lunch, or as complicated as whether or not to quit your job or leave your partner.

Practicing making decisions without consulting anyone is a great way to build self-trust and dismantle self-doubt.

WHAT TO DO

Here you're going to log small decisions you can make *without* asking others for their opinions first.

I decided...

I decided...

I decided...

I decided...

I decided...

I decided...

List What You Like about Yourself

Self-doubt can arise when you forget that there are so many things to like about yourself. You're a dynamic, interesting individual with tons of amazing qualities. Sometimes you just need a bit of a reminder, and who better than, well, *you* to do the reminding?!

WHAT TO DO

List what you like about yourself on the lines provided.

WHAT I LIKE *about Myself*

-
-
-
-
-
-
-
-
-
-
-
-

Make a Promise to Yourself to Build Self-Trust

A huge component of building self-trust is doing what you say you will—and holding yourself accountable when you happen to fall short. That said, it's always best to make promises you can keep, and that will improve your relationship with yourself. This will help you learn that you can count on yourself.

WHAT TO DO

Make a promise to yourself so you can build more self-trust and diminish self-doubt. The promise can be as small as you want; the important thing is that it should be realistic and easy to achieve. For example: "I promise I will work out tonight for at least ten minutes."

Spend Time with People Who Fill You Up

The people you spend your time with matter. If you're constantly around negative, critical humans, you're bound to become negative and critical about yourself too.

You should surround yourself with people who fill your cup and lift you up, not those who tear you down and make you feel small!

WHAT TO DO

Draw everyone who fills up your cup. This could be your mom, your best friends, your coworker . . . anyone you can think of who supports your well-being. Turn to this page whenever you need a reminder of the people who are in your corner—the ones you can call when you need a pick-me-up.

Set Up Your Day for Self-Love

You should make time for self-love every single day. There are so many daily opportunities to practice loving yourself and building up your self-confidence. It just takes a bit of planning and prioritization, that's all!

WHAT TO DO

In each of the hearts, write an item for your daily self-love to-do list. Your list can include actions and activities such as "Say my positive affirmations" or "Journal," or even "Have a spa night."

List What You Can Control

Lots of things are out of your control, but that doesn't mean you have no say in your future and your fate. Remembering the things you do have control over will make you feel more empowered, helping you go through your days with more confidence and less self-doubt.

WHAT TO DO

List everything you can think of when it comes to what you can control. For example: "I can control how I speak to myself, and I choose to speak to myself kindly."

List What You Can't Control

You're more powerful than you realize; still, there are things you don't have the power to change. Not everything is within your control, and thank goodness for that! Letting go of the things beyond your control should help take some of the pressure off you so you'll be able to focus on the things you *do* have the capability to influence.

> **WHAT TO DO**

List everything you can't control. For example: "I can't control how someone else feels about me" or "I can't control whether or not I get sick."

Schedule In More Joy

Finding time to do things you enjoy is great for building self-esteem and conquering self-doubt. It shows that you prioritize your joy and therefore yourself. That is super powerful stuff.

Of course, you're busy, and it might feel frivolous to make what some might consider "unproductive" things a priority. It's not; it's actually essential for living a balanced life! This is why you're going to take a minute right now to fit more joy into your everyday life.

WHAT TO DO

In the following boxes, schedule in one joyful activity for each day of the week. For each activity, include a specific time, what you plan to do, and how long you plan to do it. For example: "On Monday at 6 p.m., I plan to go on an hour-long walk with my dog and listen to my favorite music."

WEDNESDAY

THURSDAY

FRIDAY

SATURDAY

SUNDAY

Don't Bite Off More Than You Can Chew

When you have what feels like an insurmountable task ahead of you—or maybe many insanely large to-do list items—it can make you doubt yourself. You may convince yourself you'll never get everything done. When there's too much on your plate, you can become overwhelmed and end up feeling totally out of control and bad about yourself.

First off, take a deep breath. Then break it down so you can tackle the tough stuff ahead of you, nibble by nibble. You've got this!

WHAT TO DO

On the following page, break your big task into smaller chunks. Put the pieces in sequential order, first things first. For example, if you have a major presentation at work, your first step might be simply "create an outline for the PowerPoint deck." Then step 2 would be "make the first slide, listing the agenda," and so on.

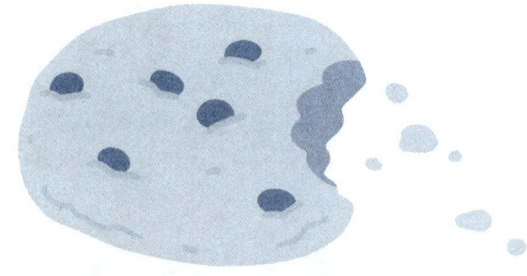

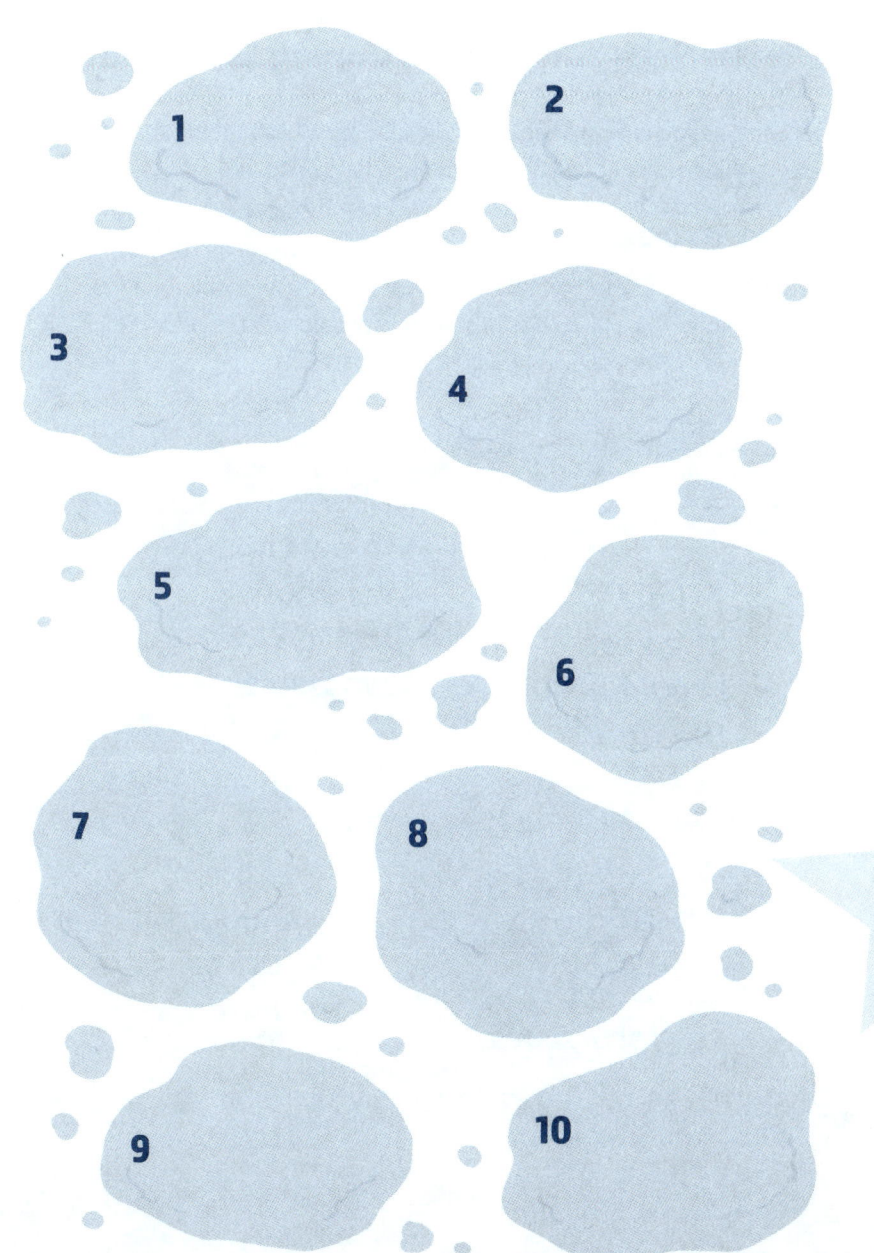

Recite Self-Compassion Coping Statements

Self-compassion is fundamental for developing a healthy self-image. You deserve your own kindness. You deserve your own love.

WHAT TO DO

Recite the following self-compassion coping statements out loud—once per statement. You can do this in a quiet room alone, in front of the mirror, or wherever you feel the most comfortable.

- I did the best I could at the time.
- Now that I know better, I can do better.
- I am worthy of forgiveness.
- I am enough just as I am.

Know Your Boundaries with Loved Ones

Healthy boundaries are an essential part of well-being. Not only do boundaries foster stronger relationships, they also keep you safe. A lack of boundaries, on the other hand, can trigger feelings of low self-worth, which can lead to self-doubt.

WHAT TO DO

Journal about what your boundaries are and how you might enforce them. Make sure to include why your boundaries exist and who you might need to set boundaries with. Some examples of healthy boundaries might be not answering texts or phone calls after a certain time of the evening, saying no without giving a lengthy explanation, or even steering clear of certain topics of conversation.

Define Success on *Your* Terms

Success is ultimately about building a life that feels good to *you*, not someone else. This means that success is not one-size-fits-all. How you define success will differ from how others define it.

WHAT TO DO

Use this space to define success based on what it would feel like for you. Don't worry about anyone else's definition. For example, would a bustling marketing career make you feel successful? Or maybe success for you involves a more family-oriented life? Perhaps it's both? Do you want to get married? Or would you rather stay single and make your friends your love story? Do you rent an apartment that you love, or purchase your dream house?

Whatever success would feel like to you, write it down. Be honest, and dream big. Because, really, success is about a life that feels like your own and no one else's.

Give Yourself Flowers

Flowers are a beautiful symbol of love, appreciation, and celebration. Salute yourself for everything you are and give *yourself* flowers! By all means you can do this literally, but you're also going to use the flowers on this page to plan an event to celebrate yourself.

WHAT TO DO

Plan out your celebration. The event can be day or night, an intimate gathering or a large affair, elaborate or informal—the important thing is that you will be the guest of honor. Within each flower, write down the details for the celebration including date, time, invitees, location, and any other related plans.

Write a Comforting Letter to Your Inner Teen

Healing your inner teen is just as important as healing your inner child. Your teenage years are deeply formative and influence much about who you are as an adult. It's during your teens that so many firsts happen, and so many ideas about who you are and who you want to become are developed. And, of course, some of those viewpoints can damage your self-image. This is why comforting your inner teen is important; it helps you heal those mindsets by acknowledging the root of the self-doubt and yanking it out.

WHAT TO DO

Think about a core memory from your teen years, one that greatly impacted your sense of self. Perhaps it was something shame-inducing, painful, or sad. Once you have your memory in mind, write a letter to your teenage self in which you explore the events surrounding the memory together.

Dear Me,

Learn to Accept a Compliment

Accepting compliments can definitely be a little uncomfortable at times, especially if you struggle with self-doubt and low self-esteem. Kind things being said about you can be difficult to believe when you don't see those qualities in yourself. With practice, though, you can learn to embrace the positive feedback and let yourself be celebrated!

WHAT TO DO

Here you're going to learn to accept a compliment; like, actually take it to heart and believe it. You can turn to this page during difficult self-love days and be reminded by the people who love you about all the good things you really are.

Write down a compliment you received recently. For example, maybe someone reminded you that you're a loyal friend. Quote exactly what the compliment giver said about you. Then thank the person for the compliment by writing down a sincere expression of gratitude for the feedback.

A COMPLIMENT I'VE RECENTLY RECEIVED

Reassure Yourself with These Affirmations

Learning how to reassure yourself in times of self-doubt is helpful for dismantling those worries and bringing yourself back to reality, allowing you to face your challenge with more clarity and confidence. Affirmations are a great way to practice reassurance, and that's where this activity can help.

WHAT TO DO

Here you'll find several self-assurance affirmations you can recite during times of need. There are also three blank spaces for you to write your own personalized self-assurance affirmations. Choose any or all that speak to your specific circumstances.

I did the best I could with the information I had at the time.

Everyone experiences self-doubt from time to time; that doesn't mean it's true.

I can do this.   *I am strong.*

_____.

_____.

_____.

Track Your Little Actions for Your Big Goals

Life moves fast—so fast sometimes it almost feels like a race. However, slow and steady wins, as they say, which is why focusing on little actions is what will ultimately serve you best in reaching your major goals. That's exactly what you're going to do here.

WHAT TO DO

On these pages, set a course of little actions you can take toward a big goal. At the finish line, write down your ultimate goal. Then, on each of the mile markers on the racetrack, list a small step you can take to reach the finish line. For example, maybe your goal is "Get a promotion." On each of the mile markers, you could write actions like "Take on more responsibility" that can help you get that new role.

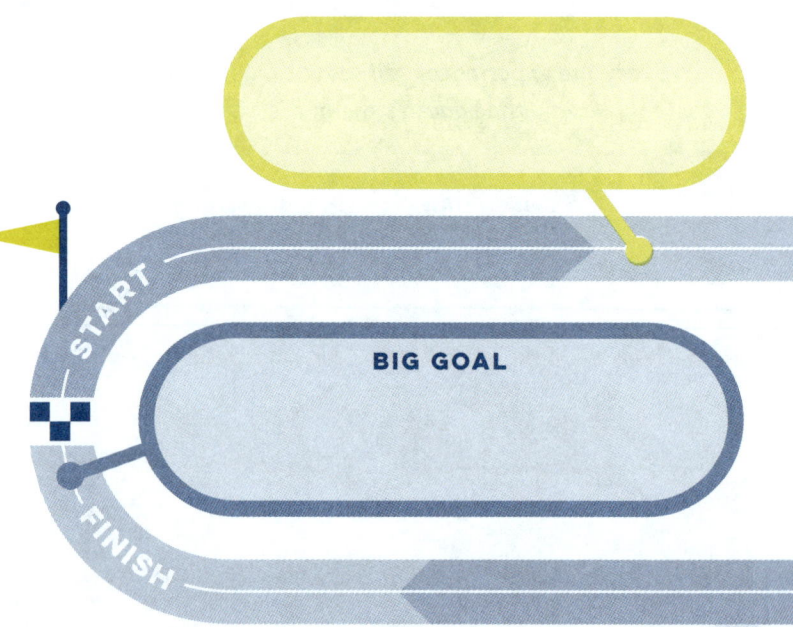

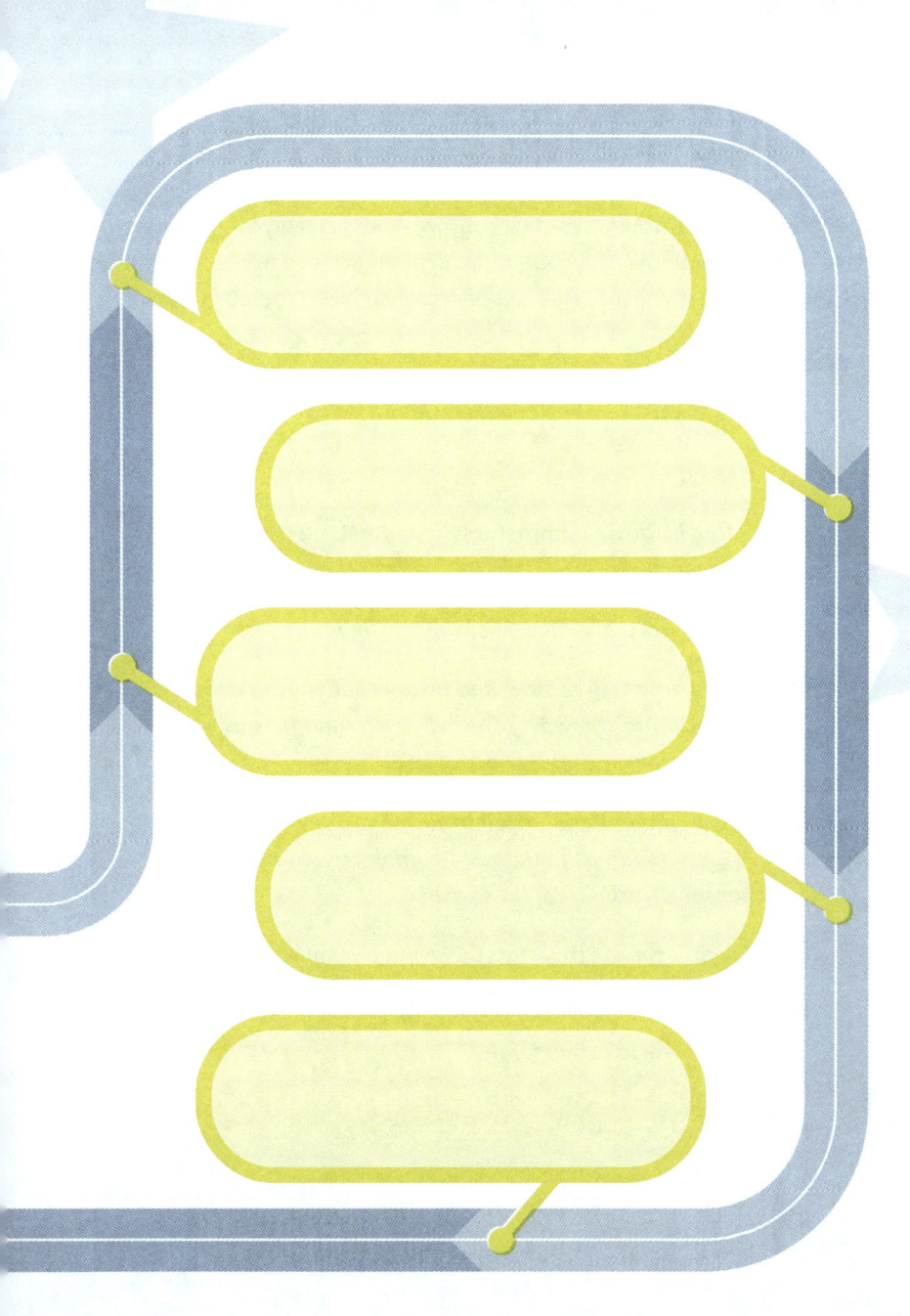

Try This Self-Acceptance Meditation

Self-acceptance is so important. After all, you can't love yourself without accepting yourself! Your strengths, your weaknesses, and everything in between come into play. Of course, it can be difficult to fully acknowledge yourself as all that you are. This self-acceptance meditation can help.

WHAT TO DO

Follow these steps to complete the meditation:

1. Sit or lie down comfortably in a quiet, distraction-free place.
2. Take a deep breath and slowly close your eyes.
3. Take three to five slow and deep breaths. Pay close attention to the way your belly rises and falls as you breathe deeply.
4. While you continue deep breathing, think to yourself, "I am enough as I am, and I completely and utterly accept myself."
5. Silently repeat this statement in your mind five times.
6. When finished, slowly open your eyes and come back to the world around you.

Practice Gratitude

Gratitude is such an important virtue to practice. Not only does gratitude help ground you in the present moment, but it can also help boost your mood and improve your life satisfaction. Paying close attention to the positive events of the day helps enhance self-esteem and strengthen your belief in yourself.

WHAT TO DO

List three things you are grateful for today:

1. _____
   _____
   _____

2. _____
   _____
   _____

3. _____
   _____
   _____

Be Nonjudgmental about Your Experience

If you're a human being, embarrassing things will occasionally happen. You'll perform in subpar ways at the function. You'll tell jokes that no one laughs at. You'll get ketchup on your white shirt. That's okay. It's time to stop judging yourself.

WHAT TO DO

Think of a memory that is causing you some self-doubt. For example, maybe you recently went on a first date and you keep replaying every "awkward" thing you said or did. Whatever your painful memory is, journal about it in the space provided. Then rewrite the details of what happened using the most neutral, nonjudgmental voice you can muster.

Remember That It's about Progress, Not Perfection

So much of life is about progress and not perfection. Small steps lead to big changes, and ultimately are what will get you to where you want and need to be. Here you're going to start taking those smaller steps.

WHAT TO DO

Write down a task that is causing you some serious self-doubt. Once you've identified what it is you need to complete, list three ways you can chip away at the daunting situation this week. Cross out each step as you complete it.

TASK:

SMALL STEPS TOWARD TASK:

1.

2.

3.

Text Your Future Self

Looking at a situation from the perspective of your future self can help you build self-trust and make good decisions. Your future self knows that you can handle whatever the current you is worried about!

WHAT TO DO

The following is an outline of a text conversation between your Current Self and your Future Self. Think about a situation you'd love your Future Self's advice on and text them about it. Respond from the vantage point of your Future Self. What advice and reassurance would they give you?

Current Self:

Future Self:

Future Self:

Current Self:

Future Self:

Reduce Your Stress with These Activities

Lowering your stress is essential for optimal mental health. Stress is associated with negative outcomes such as anxiety and depression, which can lead to low self-esteem and increased self-doubt.

WHAT TO DO

The following is a checklist of stress-reducing activities to consider trying during moments of stress. As you explore these techniques, highlight the activities that were the most helpful. This way, when stress creeps back, you can turn to this page and choose your favorite stress reliever.

- *Perform a quick yoga flow.*
- *Try deep breathing for five minutes.*
- *Color.*
- *Take a fifteen-minute reset nap.*
- *Journal.*
- *Go for a brisk walk or run outside.*
- *Do your go-to workout.*
- *Read your favorite book.*
- *Listen to uplifting music.*

Stop Selling Yourself Short

You need to stop selling yourself short. You're much more impressive than you're giving yourself credit for, and it's time to remind yourself how capable you are!

WHAT TO DO

Here you're going to write a letter of recommendation . . . for yourself! Tell the person who's hiring for your dream job just how perfect you'd be for the position. You can pick a listing on LinkedIn or even make up your own dream role. Whatever works! The point is to talk yourself up and give yourself all the credit you deserve.

To Whom It May Concern,

Sincerely, _____

Draw What Happiness Looks Like to You

Happiness looks different to everyone, which is what makes life so exciting and dynamic! There isn't one route to contentment, and that's part of the fun journey of being alive.

Of course, when you struggle with self-doubt, you may compare your definition of happiness to someone else's, making you worry that the things you love and want out of life aren't as worthy. This just isn't true though! You deserve the happiness you picture, and that's what you're going to draw here.

WHAT TO DO

On the following page, draw what happiness looks like to you. Who and what are you surrounded by? What do you do for work? For fun? Draw it all!

Do the Hard Thing First

Doing the hard thing first is a great way to counter procrastination, build self-confidence, and defeat self-doubt. When you tackle the toughest task first, it shows that you're always up for a challenge and that you trust yourself to get it done. After you do the hard part, it's all downhill!

WHAT TO DO

On a day when you have a particularly daunting to-do list, write down the most difficult thing on your list here. Then do it! After it's done, reflect on the challenge and how you rose to the occasion.

The **MOST DIFFICULT THING** *on* **MY TO-DO LIST**

Focus On What You *Really* Want

What do you want out of life? No, not what your parents, or society, or your BFF want for you. What do *you* want? If anything was possible and it was bound to work out, what would you go for? What kind of job would you have? Where would you live? What kind of partner would you have or not have? Here you're going to explore the answers to these questions.

WHAT TO DO

Journal about what you want to experience while you're here on earth. Be honest with yourself!

Reconnect with Your Inner Voice

Your inner voice is your compass. It's the basis of your self-trust, guiding you through life with confidence, assuredness, and self-respect. Sometimes, though, the noise around you can get pretty loud; other people's opinions, your own worries, and stress can all lead you to lose touch with your inner voice. Well, it's time for you to reconnect with your inner voice once again. This will help you rebuild your sense of self, trust yourself more, and ultimately build up your self-esteem.

WHAT TO DO

Here you're going to get back in touch with your inner voice through a visualization exercise. Follow the steps below so you'll remember how to block out whatever may distract you from trusting the instinctive guidance that is your birthright.

1. *Sit or lie down comfortably in a quiet place.*

2. *Close your eyes. This will help remove distractions around you and help you go inward, giving you a better chance to hear your inner voice.*

3. *Take five deep breaths. Pay close attention to the way your belly rises and falls as you breathe. Really step back into your body, feeling every sensation.*

4. *While you continue deep breathing, invite yourself inward. Imagine walking through the hallways of your heart, following the echo of your inner voice, letting it guide you back home to yourself.*

5. *Slowly open your eyes to end the practice.*

Reframe the Failure

Reframing an error, rather than punishing yourself and feeling bad about yourself, is a much better way to respond to a setback. Reframing means looking at your mistake differently. For example, let's say your boss sent back a project you drafted, and it's covered with marked-up corrections. Instead of thinking that you really screwed up, you can reframe your response by seeing the situation as a great opportunity to learn from your boss's feedback.

WHAT TO DO

Use this space to journal about an error and how it can be reframed as something positive:

Take a Breath

Breath work is a great way to settle down and bring yourself back into your body when you're feeling doubtful about yourself and your abilities. Many different types of breath work exercises are available to help you calm down. One popular technique is known as box breathing.

WHAT TO DO

Follow these steps for box breathing to ground yourself back in your body when self-doubt tries to take over:

1. *Sit comfortably in a quiet, distraction-free place.*
2. *Take a deep breath through your nose, counting to 4 as you inhale.*
3. *Hold your breath, counting to 4 as you do so.*
4. *Once you reach 4, slowing start to breathe out through your mouth. As you exhale, count to 4.*
5. *Hold your breath to the count of 4.*
6. *Begin the cycle again on your next inhale, and repeat several times.*

Do One Thing for Your Future Self Today

Keeping your future self in mind is important for living well in the present, making mindful choices that will benefit you long term. This helps you avoid feeling disappointed in yourself and ultimately leads to good decision-making—so you can feel confident in your choices.

WHAT TO DO

Use the space provided to plan one thing you can do today that your future self will be grateful that you did now. For example: "I will clean my kitchen before bed so it's spotless for tomorrow morning when I wake up."

Plan a Self-Care Day

Self-care isn't a luxury; it's an absolute necessity. Attending to your personal needs shows that you value your well-being and therefore yourself. Self-care is a crucial component of wellness, self-love, and health.

WHAT TO DO

Plan a self-care day in detail. Schedule the exact date and time, and list the activities you will do to take better care of yourself. For example: "This Sunday, I will dedicate the day starting at 10 a.m. to self-care such as eating a healthy breakfast, working out, practicing meditation, cleaning my home, and listening to a self-development podcast."

List Your Needs

Knowing your needs is important so that you're able to meet them for yourself, as well as communicate them to the people in your life. When you make sure your needs are met you can dismantle self-doubt because it shows that you know and respect yourself.

WHAT TO DO

List your needs and brainstorm ways in which they can be met each and every day. Differentiate between personal needs and social needs.

Explore Your Values

Values are personal beliefs that create your internal compass. Your values guide you through life, helping you to assess what is valuable, worthwhile, and most true to you. This ultimately informs your behavior and the way you move through the world. Values can include things such as integrity, honesty, loyalty, kindness, social justice, and fairness.

Sticking to your values is a great way to practice self-respect and establish self-trust. The first step is to identify your values.

WHAT TO DO

Here, you're going to list five of your main values and brainstorm ways you can practice these values in your everyday life. For example, if "kindness" is one of your values, you can write something like: "I value kindness, which means I will always do my best to act from a place of compassion and nonjudgment when it comes to interacting with others and myself."

MY VALUES	HOW I CAN PRACTICE THIS VALUE

MY VALUES	HOW I CAN PRACTICE THIS VALUE

Embrace Your Imperfections

You're human, which means you are imperfect by design. You'll have flaws and shortcomings and say the wrong thing at times. You will run late.

WHAT TO DO

This exercise will help you embrace your imperfections through mindfulness, specifically visualization. Don't let the pursuit of perfection make you doubt yourself. You can learn to roll with the tiny flaws that make you the unique human you are. Just follow these steps:

1. *Sit or lie down comfortably in a quiet place.*

2. *Close your eyes. This will help you ignore any distractions and help you go inward.*

3. *Take five deep breaths. Pay close attention to the way your belly rises and falls.*

4. *Continue deep breathing, and as you do, imagine your imperfections as your friends at a dinner table. Consider how each of them is important to you in some way, and how you couldn't feel like yourself without them.*

5. *Finally, thank everyone for coming to the table.*

6. *Slowly open your eyes as you exhale to end the practice.*

Measure Your Worth Differently

When it comes to self-worth, we often turn to external attributes such as our bank balance and position on the corporate ladder to measure success and status. However, no matter what, you are inherently worthy. It's time to measure your worth with different metrics.

WHAT TO DO

Fill in each of the blanks to help you measure your worth differently and see how amazing you truly are. For example, for the first prompt, you could say you're wealthy because you're rich in character.

I am wealthy, not because of my bank account but because _____ .

I am successful, not because of my job but because _____ .

I am pretty, not because of the number on the scale but because _____ .

I am likable, not because of what I can do for others but because _____ .

Remember That You Can't Do It All (And That's Okay)

While you definitely should have faith in yourself, that doesn't mean you have to be everything to everyone. It's important to maintain realistic expectations, for both yourself and the people in your life. There are some things you just won't be able to accomplish during this lifetime, and that's no problem!

WHAT TO DO

Write yourself a reminder about why it's okay that you can't do it all. Be kind to yourself, and think of the positives of not being able to be everything all the time.

Do a Social Media Comparison Cleanse

Social media is a great way to stay connected, but it's also a great place to get caught in the comparison trap and begin to doubt yourself. This is why you're going to do a social media comparison cleanse.

WHAT TO DO

Go through this checklist of social media platforms and reflect on whether any of the accounts you may follow make you doubt yourself. Then unfollow or mute those accounts. If there are other platforms you subscribe to, include them on the blank spaces and unfollow or mute any that make you doubt yourself.

- [ ] *Instagram*
- [ ] *X*
- [ ] *Facebook*
- [ ] *TikTok*
- [ ] *LinkedIn*
- [ ] *Snapchat*
- [ ] *YouTube*
- [ ] _____
- [ ] _____
- [ ] _____

Give Yourself More Credit

You're doing so much better than you think you are. Don't believe it? You're going to remind yourself of your greatness right here, right now. Get ready to give yourself the credit you deserve, at long last!

WHAT TO DO

In each of the outlines provided, write down attributes you like about yourself, accomplishments you've achieved lately, and so on. This will help show you that you're doing so much better than you think you are.

Build Yourself Up

Rebuilding your self-esteem can feel difficult, but making the effort is definitely worth it. You deserve to feel good about yourself! You deserve to feel good things! You deserve to live your life free from self-doubt!

WHAT TO DO

It's time to build yourself up, brick by brick. In each of the bricks, write down one small action you can take that will help foster your self-esteem. Thes actions could be anything from signing up for a new workout class to getting a massage to wearing your favorite outfit that makes you feel confident.

Consider a Different Perspective

Looking at your life and yourself from a different perspective can be helpful for problem-solving, reframing, and even conquering self-doubt. When you look at a difficult situation or yourself from another's vantage point, you might see things you missed at first.

WHAT TO DO

Think about a difficult situation or a negative belief you have about yourself. Then write about it from the perspective of a friend or family member. Consider how they'd talk to you and how they'd advise you about this particular aspect of your life.

Set Realistic Expectations

Setting realistic expectations is essential; otherwise, you could be setting yourself up for failure. When you overcommit or impose unrealistic deadlines on yourself, it's almost a self-fulfilling prophecy—one that says you're a failure and never do anything right.

WHAT TO DO

Here you're going to explore how to establish specific expectations around something you're working toward. On the following page, fill in the blanks to create achievable guidelines for your efforts to reach your goal. Answer each question honestly.

The goal:

_____
_____
_____
_____
_____

When it's due:

_____
_____
_____

How much time I realistically have to commit to this goal:

Is there any buffer time I can add?

What are some potential obstacles I might face?

Finish These Self-Awareness Statements

Self-awareness is key for developing self-confidence. The better you know yourself, the more you can trust yourself. Self-doubt will take a back seat, and you'll feel empowered to face challenges and live your very best life.

WHAT TO DO

Finish each of the following self-awareness statements so you can get to know yourself better and be more accepting of everything that you are.

I am good at _____
_____.

I am not so good at _____
_____.

I could try harder at _____
_____.

My best quality is _____
_____.

My worst quality is _____
_____.

My purpose is _____
_____.

Say These Self-Worth Affirmations

Establishing self-worth is a great way to dismantle self-doubt—and one way to foster more self-worth is through affirmations! Here you're going to recite some suggested self-worth affirmations as well as come up with your own.

WHAT TO DO

Sit or lie down comfortably in a quiet, distraction-free place. Then recite one, some, or all the self-worth affirmations listed here. Repeat the statements until you start believing them. When you're done, try your hand at writing a few self-worth affirmations of your own to really drive home the point that you are worthy! Repeat these affirmations any time you feel self-doubt creeping back.

I am inherently worthy.

I always matter.

I am enough.

I did the best I could.

Be Mindful of Your Self-Doubt Catchphrases

We all have standard negative self-talk expressions we turn to when full of self-doubt. For example: "I will never get this done" or "Why did I think I could accomplish this?" Knowing your self-doubt catchphrases helps you notice them in the moment and recognize them for what they are revealing: insecurity, not reality. Understanding that sometimes your thoughts are just that—thoughts—will allow you to take your power back.

WHAT TO DO

Here you're going to identify your self-doubt catchphrases. In the space provided, write down phrases you habitually repeat to yourself when you're doubting yourself the most. For example: "I never am good enough."

Embrace That You're Not Everyone's Cup of Tea

A fact of life: You are not for everyone. That's just fine, because not everyone is for you either! This is why finding your people and the places where you belong is so important; feeling like you actually fit in doesn't happen everywhere. Surrounding yourself with people who love you and spending time at tables where you'll always have a seat is imperative for building yourself up and banishing self-doubt. This exercise will help you better understand why your comfort zone is what it is.

WHAT TO DO

Within each cup of tea, write down a reason why you're glad you aren't for everyone. For example: "I'm glad I'm not for everyone because that means I'm living a more authentic life."

Fail Forward

"Failing forward" is a powerfully positive mindset that looks at failure as simply part of the journey. When you fail forward, you see detours as lessons and setbacks as information you can use to keep moving toward your goals and do better next time.

Failing forward is a great strategy for conquering self-doubt because it doesn't look at mistakes as roadblocks but rather as jumping-off points, pushing away any feelings of defeat and keeping momentum and motivation intact.

WHAT TO DO

You're going to practice failing forward by focusing on the new information you acquired from a mistake. You'll use what you've learned to help you make a more informed and educated choice the next time you're faced with a similar situation.

Answer the following prompts to reflect on what you learned and how you can use this intel to move—and fail—forward.

Describe the situation:

_____
_____
_____
_____
_____
_____
_____

What went wrong?

_____
_____
_____
_____
_____
_____

What new vantage points did you acquire through these missteps?

_____
_____
_____
_____
_____
_____
_____

How will you use this new information next time?

_____
_____
_____
_____
_____
_____
_____

Draw a Self-Portrait

Sometimes you need to see yourself from the perspective of someone who adores you so you can see yourself more clearly. There's a reason why self-love advice like "Talk to yourself the way someone who loves you would" is so popular! It definitely builds self-esteem.

WHAT TO DO

Draw a self-portrait as if it was your best friend drawing you. Think about how they view you. What are their favorite things about you? What do they compliment you on the most? Your BFF's love for you will shine through in your portrait and help you embrace your self-worth!

Improve Your Self-Image

Looking at yourself from a positive perspective is a great way to improve your self-image. And that's exactly what you're going to do here.

WHAT TO DO

In this activity, you'll see various mirrors. Within each mirror, illustrate a quality that you think of as one of your best. For example: In the first mirror, you could draw yourself being kind. In the second, you might show yourself being strong. And so on. This exercise will serve as a reminder of everything that you are, not what you lack.

Understand Impostor Syndrome

If you experience pervasive uncertainty and doubt about your abilities, talents, and accomplishments, you may be suffering from impostor syndrome. This mindset causes you to believe that your achievements are flukes rather than the result of your hard work or talent. You may constantly feel on edge, worried about being exposed as the "impostor" you think you are.

In addition to being totally exhausting, impostor syndrome is related to other issues (e.g., perfectionism, burnout, reduced motivation, procrastination) that can seriously affect your personal and professional lives.

WHAT TO DO

This exercise will help you understand how your impostor syndrome manifests so you can recognize it and defeat it. Follow the prompts to uncover more about impostor syndrome and the ways it impacts your life.

Once you see your impostor syndrome for what it is, you'll be able to take its power away.

In which areas of your life do you feel like an impostor? (For example, work, relationships, hobbies, etc.)

_____
_____
_____
_____
_____
_____

Describe the specific circumstances that led to a recent bout of impostor syndrome. (For example, did you get a raise at work and feel like you didn't deserve it?)

_____
_____
_____

Why did you feel like a fraud in this scenario?

_____
_____
_____

What contradictory evidence is there that supports that you do deserve the praise or accomplishment?

_____
_____
_____

Write a positive statement to yourself affirming that you are worthy of the success you've experienced. Even if it doesn't feel true or if you feel awkward, do your best to be as confident as possible in what you write. You deserve good things!

_____
_____
_____

Track Your Progress

Tracking your progress not only helps you see how far you have to go, but it also helps you see how much you've already done!

> **WHAT TO DO**

Here, you're going to track your progress toward a few of your goals. This exercise is a good way to show yourself that you've accomplished more than you think, and that there's no reason to doubt your ability to achieve whatever you put your mind to.

THE GOAL:

DATE I STARTED: / /

WHERE I STARTED:

WHAT I'VE ACCOMPLISHED:

WHAT I CAN DO NEXT:

THE GOAL:

DATE I STARTED: / /

WHERE I STARTED:

WHAT I'VE ACCOMPLISHED:

WHAT I CAN DO NEXT:

THE GOAL:

DATE I STARTED: / /

WHERE I STARTED:

WHAT I'VE ACCOMPLISHED:

WHAT I CAN DO NEXT:

THE GOAL:

DATE I STARTED: / /

WHERE I STARTED:

WHAT I'VE ACCOMPLISHED:

WHAT I CAN DO NEXT:

Ask Your Younger Self for Advice

We're often asked to think about how our future selves might advise us to navigate through a difficult situation or choice. But our younger selves can have powerful perspectives too. That's why you're going to ask your younger self for advice now. This exercise will help dim self-doubt because it will remind you of who you are at your core.

WHAT TO DO

Use the space provided to reflect on a specific scenario in your life that you need some guidance on. For example, maybe you need to tell a friend they hurt your feelings. Writing in the voice of the younger you, describe what you'd say under the circumstances of your chosen scenario.

Don't Overcommit

Overcommitting is self-sabotage. It's a way to overwhelm yourself and make you believe you're not capable of doing hard things. But you *are*! You just need to be intentional about how much you take on at once.

WHAT TO DO

You're going to commit to not overcommitting right now by signing a contract with yourself that clearly states you will not overcommit:

MY NAME:

DATE: /   /

I promise to not overcommit to things that are not realistically possible.

MY SIGNATURE:

Try Loving-Kindness Meditation

Loving-kindness meditation, also known as metta meditation, is all about cultivating goodwill and compassion toward both yourself and others. This practice involves silently repeating loving phrases to yourself as you meditate. Metta meditation will help diminish your self-doubt because it's an act of loving-kindness toward yourself, reinforcing self-love and confidence in yourself.

WHAT TO DO

To perform loving-kindness meditation, follow the steps on the following page.

1. Sit or lie down comfortably in a quiet, distraction-free place.

2. Close your eyes. You can also choose to simply relax your gaze.

3. Bring a loved one to mind, someone who has impacted your life in a positive way. Feel your being filled with feelings of warmth and love for that person.

4. Begin silently repeating phrases of love and acceptance toward yourself.

5. Direct those feelings of love and support to others.

6. Extend those feelings to everyone in the world.

7. Conclude the practice by saying three expressions of gratitude out loud. Then, open your eyes.

Practice Self-Forgiveness

Sometimes the hardest person to forgive is yourself. But self-forgiveness is one of the most important things you can do for yourself. You are stuck with you for your whole life; it's so much easier if you make yourself a friend rather than a foe. Plus, forgiving yourself is foundational for building self-trust and a positive sense of self.

Dear Me,

WHAT TO DO

On these pages, you're going to write two letters to yourself. For the first, you will apologize to yourself. You can be saying sorry for something specific or making a general all-purpose apology. For the second, you will write a response of forgiveness.

Dear Me,

Do Something for Someone Else

Often the best thing you can do for yourself is to take your mind off yourself by doing something kind for another person. Not only does this help build healthy relationships and foster positive interactions, but it also just feels good to be helpful! Plus, that's always great for building confidence too. It's a win-win!

WHAT TO DO

You're going to plan an act of kindness for a loved one. Provide the details by filling in the blanks.

Who:

What I'll do:

When I'll do it:

How I felt afterward:

Set Five Small Goals to Accomplish This Week

Setting small goals is an excellent way to build self-trust and prove to yourself that you are capable and competent. That's why you're going to plan to complete five mini tasks this week.

WHAT TO DO

In the space provided, list five small goals you can achieve this week. These could include things as simple as doing a load of laundry, completing that return you've been putting off, or even doing two workouts at the gym. Once you're done, check off the goal to signify it's complete.

☐ GOAL 1

☐ GOAL 2

☐ GOAL 3

☐ GOAL 4

☐ GOAL 5

Consider the Source

We all receive feedback every now and then, but it's always worth considering the source of both positive and negative feedback. Some people's perspectives just don't serve you, aren't honest, or aren't realistic. Therefore, you should always vet the comments you receive about yourself and your life.

WHAT TO DO

Here you're going to consider the source of some recent feedback, whether it was positive or negative. Then you're going to determine if the feedback is worth taking into consideration, based on what you know about the source.

The source: _____

The feedback: _____

_____

_____

Worthy feedback? **YES** or **NO** *(CIRCLE ONE!)*

Why or why not?: _____

_____

_____

_____

_____

List Three Good Decisions You've Made in the Past

You're not the hot mess you've convinced yourself that you are. You've made plenty of good choices in the past that have helped you reach some pretty cool places. That's what you're going to remind yourself of right now.

WHAT TO DO

List three good decisions you've made in the past. It could be something as big as the college you chose or as small as the healthy lunch you chose to eat today.

My GOOD DECISIONS

1 _____
_____
_____

2 _____
_____
_____

3 _____
_____
_____

Make an Action Plan

If you're doubting yourself, sometimes it's because you have a major goal ahead of you that feels impossible to reach. That's why you're going to make an action plan to help you overcome your self-doubt and work toward your goal.

WHAT TO DO

Fill in the prompts to clarify your goal and its challenges. Then, make a step-by-step plan for how you're going to achieve your goal.

PREPARE

My big goal: _____

When I want to achieve it by: __/__/__

Challenges I might face: _____

How I can mitigate these challenges: _____

PLAN

STEP 1

STEP 2

STEP 3

STEP 4

STEP 5

Build Self-Esteem with These Activities

In some ways, self-esteem is like a muscle. You need to exercise it, condition it, and work on increasing its power the same as you would, say, your quads. The more you practice building self-esteem, the stronger it gets!

There are many activities that will be helpful to incorporate into your self-esteem "workout." You'll explore a few here.

WHAT TO DO

On the following page is a checklist of activities that are great for building self-esteem. In moments of self-doubt, try one (or several) of these to give yourself a boost. Highlight the activities that you find to be most helpful so you can return to them whenever self-doubt strikes.

- Journal about something you accomplished recently.
- Write about a time you felt self-assured.
- List your personal strengths.
- Do a workout you enjoy.
- Practice gratitude by writing down three things you're grateful for in the present moment.
- Dance.
- Do something you're good at.
- Work on building a new skill.
- Establish personal goals, big or small.
- Take a long, hot shower.
- Clean your bedroom.
- Find a cause you care about and get involved in volunteering.
- Say positive affirmations in front of the mirror.
- Do something outside of your comfort zone.

Create a Self-Compassion Log

Being kind to yourself is so important. You can't berate yourself into being a better person, and you certainly can't be cruel to yourself and expect to believe in yourself! Learning how to practice self-compassion can help.

WHAT TO DO

Write down all the ways you've practiced self-compassion lately. Can't come up with any? That's okay! Instead, write down instances where you could have given yourself more kindness, and brainstorm ways you'll be more compassionate toward yourself the next time.

Quit Comparing Yourself

We've all been there: You scroll through your social media feed and all of a sudden thirty minutes have passed and your friends' glowing posts have got you feeling like a loser. Five people are engaged, two got promoted, and another just went on an epic trip to Greece. Soon enough, you start wondering why them and not you, and ultimately you start doubting that you deserve those things too.

This is a classic comparison trap, but remember that comparison isn't doing you any favors. It just makes you feel bad, and it's not serving you. Frankly, it never really did at all! That's why you're finally going to quit comparing yourself to others.

WHAT TO DO

Write a resignation letter to comparing yourself to others. Be specific about why this role is not serving you and how you will be moving on to bigger and better things.

Find More Balance

Balance means you're living in a way that feels aligned with good health. It means you're not overextending yourself; you're only taking on what is truly possible, giving you peace of mind and steadiness. Living from a place of balance helps lower stress, meaning you feel more grounded and capable to take on challenges. A balanced life is a life well lived, and one that you can be confident in living.

WHAT TO DO

Think about all the ways you feel a sense of imbalance in your life. Perhaps it's a conflict related to balancing work demands with time spent on your personal life. On either side of the seesaw on the following page, write down ways you can balance those competing areas of your life. For example, maybe you're taking on too much at work without proper compensation. Or perhaps a friend is treating you like an emotional dumping ground without giving much emotional support for your own challenges in return.

Be More Aware of Yourself

Self-awareness helps you know yourself better and therefore trust yourself more too. Here you're going to do an exercise that helps you become more aware of yourself.

WHAT TO DO

Fill in these prompts to increase your self-awareness.

My strengths:

_____

_____

My weaknesses:

_____

_____

My room for growth:

_____

_____

How my best friend would describe me:

_____

_____

How a stranger might describe me:

_____

_____

Be Grateful for Your Shortcomings

You might not always realize it, but there's so much to be grateful for when it comes to your shortcomings. For example, let's say a friend called you out because you were not giving them your full attention when they were venting about a problem. Instead of shame-spiraling and thinking you're a terrible friend, you could think, "Wow, they respect our friendship enough to communicate with me. I'm lucky! And I can do better next time." You're going to journal here about these silver linings in your shortcomings.

WHAT TO DO

Write down the positives of recent shortcomings (or shortcomings from the past that you keep returning to).

Challenge Your Negative Thoughts

In addition to replacing your negative thoughts with positive ones (see Replace Your Negative Self-Talk with Positive Self-Talk), challenging the negative thoughts is another great way to make them lose their power over you. Minus the negativity, you'll be able to operate from a more positive and self-assured place. This exercise will help get you there.

WHAT TO DO

Identify any recurrent negative thoughts you have. Write down each thought and then write a statement that challenges the thought, arguing against why it isn't actually true. For example, a common negative thought might be: "I always mess everything up." The challenge, then, could be: "I make mistakes, but that's not all I do. I've had plenty of success too."

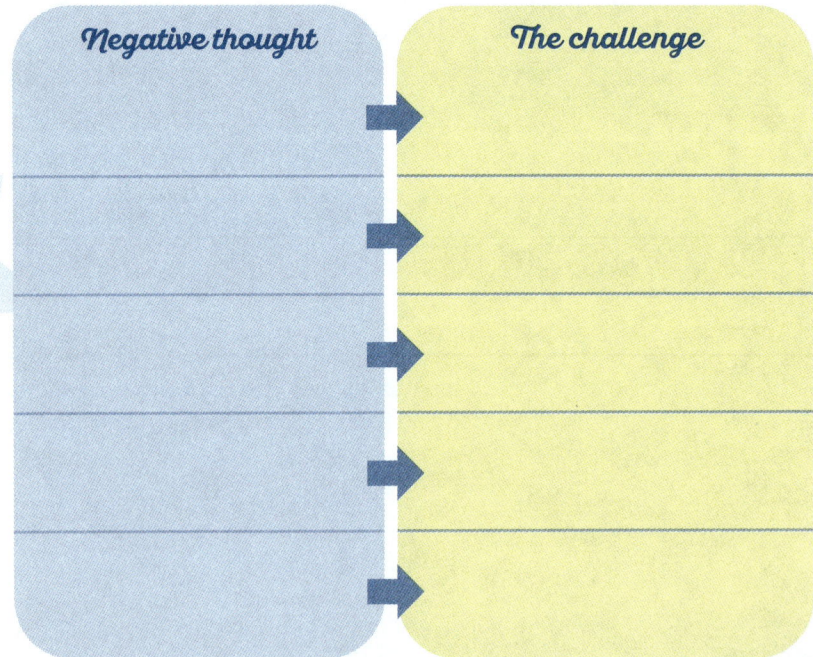

Be Your Own Best Friend

Being your own best friend means you have your own back. You move through life and act according to your own best interests. You take care of yourself, you take responsibility, and most importantly, you believe in yourself. When you are your own best friend you can dismantle self-doubt because you're able to view yourself as you would a loved one, and to treat yourself with that care.

WHAT TO DO

You're going to practice being your own best friend through mindfulness. Follow these steps:

1. Sit or lie down comfortably in a quiet, distraction-free place.

2. Close your eyes and take three deep breaths. Pay close attention to the way your belly rises and falls as you breathe.

3. While you continue deep breathing, imagine that you're sitting next to yourself. Feel how calm you are in your own presence; you are your own best friend after all!

4. Keep embracing that calm, self-assured feeling for ten minutes.

5. Open your eyes and continue your day, knowing your best friend is always with you.

Chase Your Dreams

When you struggle with self-doubt, it might seem easier to just put your dreams on the back burner because you're convinced you're not capable of achieving them. Well, you're wrong; you are worthy of your dreams! You deserve to go after them, and you're going to take the first steps here and now.

WHAT TO DO

In each of the clouds, write down one of the top five dreams you have for your life. Then explain why you're worthy of chasing that dream.

Try Something Again

Just because you don't succeed at something the first time you try it, that doesn't mean you won't ever get it down; it's always worth trying something again!

WHAT TO DO

In this activity, you're going to try something again and journal about the experience. Maybe you attempted a new skill in the past and were not immediately successful. Give it another go! This is great for challenging self-doubt because it shows you're willing to give yourself a second chance to succeed, even if it's hard.

Acknowledge How Far You've Come

Sometimes it's difficult to see how far you've come and how much you've truly accomplished. Perhaps you had a bit of trouble listing past wins in earlier activities in this workbook. But think about it like this: Your past self would be proud and in awe if they could see you now! Wow—look at you go! This is why you're going to shift perspectives and acknowledge how far you've come and how much progress you've already made.

WHAT TO DO

On the following page, write yourself a letter from the perspective of your past self, seeing your current self and everything you've achieved. Have your past self talk about where you are career-wise, in your friendships, your love life, your health, whatever you want!

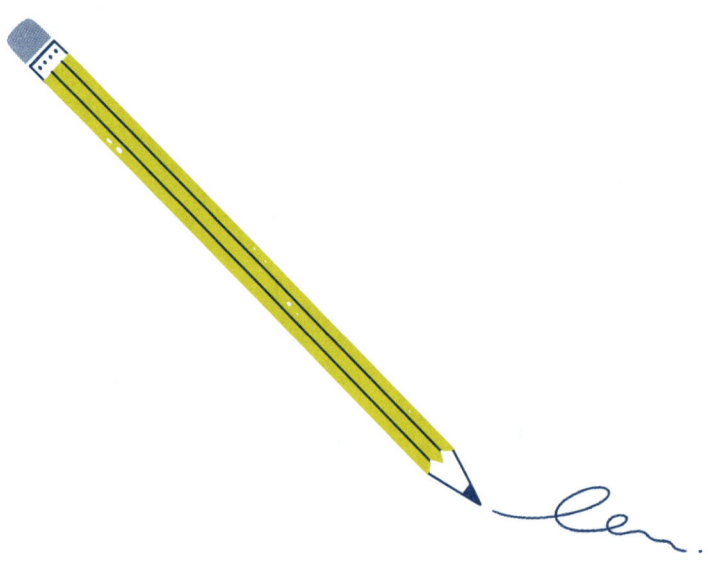

Develop a Growth Mindset

The term "growth mindset" was coined by Stanford professor Carol Dweck and it's all about the belief that you can develop skills and intelligence through hard work and dedication. A growth mindset is linked to greater adaptability, higher achievements, and enhanced motivation, all of which are great for conquering self-doubt!

WHAT TO DO

You're going to work on developing a growth mindset in this activity by looking at challenges as stepping stones. In each stepping stone provided, write down what you can gain from a current challenge.

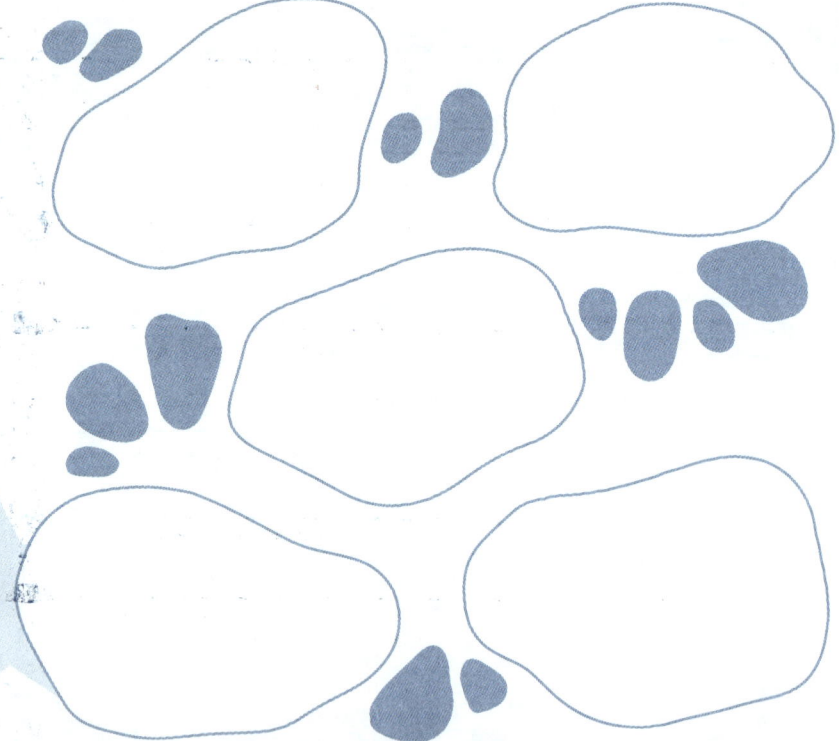

Draw a Vision Board of Your Hopes

Vision boards can be helpful tools when it comes to getting your goals and aspirations in order. Not only do they create a clear picture of the type of life you want to live, they also can inspire you and help you stay focused.

WHAT TO DO

Draw a vision board of your hopes. These can be related to your career, your relationships, your health—anything really! Feel free to find inspirational images online to help spur your imagination, and dream big.

Stop Judging Yourself

You are truly your own worst critic. No one is judging you as harshly as you are judging yourself. So why not let yourself off the hook every now and then? You deserve your own grace. You deserve to be kind to yourself. You deserve to be free of judgment.

WHAT TO DO

In each speech bubble provided, give a reason for why the judge (you) is letting you off with a kind warning. For example: "I find you not guilty of being the worst person ever because you forgot your homework again. I encourage you to slow down in the morning and make sure you packed your backpack next time. Dismissed!"

Repeat These Self-Acceptance Affirmations

Self-acceptance requires that you be honest with yourself and kind at the same time. It also means knowing that you aren't perfect; you're human! When you accept yourself as you are, you acknowledge that mistakes will happen, and you're still worthy anyway. By practicing self-acceptance, you foster self-love, which can help increase your self-esteem and diminish self-doubt.

WHAT TO DO

The following is a list of self-acceptance affirmations that will inspire you to take yourself as everything that you are, love yourself more, and ultimately show self-doubt the door. Repeat these self-acceptance affirmations out loud whenever you need a boost. You can also write your own self-acceptance affirmations on the last three lines.

I am worthy of love and respect, even when I make a mistake.

I matter.   *I am inherently enough.*

My feelings are valid, even if others don't necessarily understand.

I embrace every part of myself.

_____.

_____.

_____.

Validate Your Feelings

Validating your feelings is a major component of both emotional intelligence and self-respect. When you acknowledge your feelings and treat them as worthwhile, you're giving yourself permission to exist as all that you are. It also helps you to work through self-doubt so you can face uncomfortable feelings with grace and resilience.

WHAT TO DO

Here you're going to use mindfulness to remind yourself that the things you feel are valid. Follow these steps to complete the exercise:

1. *Sit or lie down comfortably in a quiet, distraction-free place.*

2. *Close your eyes. Take three deep breaths, in through your nose and then out through your mouth.*

3. *As you feel yourself relax, think (or say out loud): "My feelings matter because I matter. I should never doubt my own worth." Repeat these statements three to five times. Let them really sink in.*

4. *Slowly open your eyes and take one more deep breath, in through your nose and then out through your mouth.*

Cut Yourself Some Slack

When you fall short, sometimes the only thing you can really do is cut yourself some slack. Life is difficult, and that will never not be true. You're going to have hard days; you're going to have hard weeks, or even months. You're human, after all! Remembering current vulnerabilities is a great way to take failure less personally and remind yourself that life gets in the way sometimes, and that's okay.

WHAT TO DO

You're going to cut yourself some slack. Think of a recent "failure." Now, write about what else was going on in your life that maybe prevented you from giving that thing your full attention and effort.

Create a Self-Esteem Night Routine

How you end your day matters a lot when it comes to fostering good self-esteem. You can use this time to reflect on what you did well, what you could have done better, and how you might improve moving forward. This can solidify self-confidence and dismantle self-doubt.

WHAT TO DO

Schedule your evening routine to include some tasks that will boost your self-esteem. Setting specific times will make it easier to follow the schedule.

TIME:	TASK:
TIME:	TASK:
TIME:	TASK:
TIME:	TASK:
TIME:	TASK:
TIME:	TASK:

Choose Yourself

You deserve to choose yourself. To put yourself first. To love yourself. And that's what you're going to remind yourself of right now.

WHAT TO DO

Fill out these prompts to help you choose yourself:

I choose myself because:

_____
_____
_____
_____

I deserve to choose myself because:

_____
_____
_____
_____

It's okay to put myself first sometimes because:

_____
_____
_____
_____

Draw Your Most Confident Self

Despite what you might feel right now, a confident version of yourself does exist. You just need to invite them out of hiding!

WHAT TO DO

In the space provided, draw the most confident version of yourself. What kind of work do they do? Who are their friends? What aspects of themselves do they nurture? How do they take care of themself? What do they do to unwind? Have fun? Relax? Draw it all!

Be the Hero of Your Own Story

You are the hero of your own story. You can save yourself; you can get yourself through your toughest moments; and you are capable of rising from the rubble.

WHAT TO DO

Journal about all the ways you've been your own hero lately. If you can't think of any, brainstorm about how you can be your own hero in the future.

Practice Assertive Communication

Assertive communication means sharing your thoughts and feelings in a way that is direct, clear, and respectful to yourself and the person you are communicating with. For example, maybe a friend always cancels plans last minute, which makes you feel disrespected. Instead of being passive-aggressive or snapping at them, you might say the following if you were practicing assertive communication: "Hi, I know things come up and life is busy, but I feel as though you cancel last minute a lot, which makes me feel that my time is not respected. Can we work on honoring our plans moving forward?" Practicing assertive communication is great for fostering positive relationships with others and building self-respect.

However, if you struggle with self-doubt, you might be wary of assertive communication because you have trouble with standing up for yourself, speaking up for your needs, or simply expressing your opinions on a situation. Assertive communication might even feel aggressive, but this is simply not the case. There's nothing wrong with standing up for yourself, your beliefs, and your needs! That's why you're going to practice assertive communication right now by using "I" statements.

WHAT TO DO

First, think of a recent interpersonal situation that was difficult. For example, a "joke" your friend made that felt more like an insult. Once you have your scenario in mind, write out some clear, concise, and direct "I" statements that clearly state your perspective. Begin with, for example: "I need . . ." or "I feel . . ." or "I felt . . ."

Get Organized with These Tasks

A cluttered space is a sure sign of a messy mind. That internal chaos can lead to anxiety which, in turn, can facilitate feelings of self-doubt. This is why getting organized and cleaning up your physical surroundings can be helpful for starting fresh and getting a grip.

WHAT TO DO

If you're noticing that the clutter, mess, and general lack of tidiness in your home is getting out of hand, it's time to do a little house cleaning! Getting everything back in order will help you reset physically as well as mentally!

On the following page, you'll see a list of organizational tasks related to straightening up your home. Make a plan to tackle as many as you can. You might schedule a few tasks on different days if that feels more manageable, or you could simply complete whichever list items feel most relevant right now.

- Make your bed.
- Change your sheets.
- Do one load of laundry.
- Clean out your refrigerator.
- Wash your dishes (and put them away!).
- Declutter one junk drawer.
- Sort through a closet.
- Scrub your bathroom.
- Go through your loose papers.
- Donate items.
- Dust.
- Vacuum.
- Clean your windows.

Reroute Self-Critical Thoughts

As you learned in an earlier activity, negative self-talk will wear down your self-confidence over time. Self-criticism might at times feel like self-honesty, but usually when you're talking down to yourself, you aren't really addressing the full story. While taking accountability for your actions is one thing, completely disregarding your vulnerabilities, the effort you have made, and any current circumstances isn't always simply radical honesty; rather, it might be that you're just being mean to yourself.

Self-criticism is also a breeding ground for self-doubt! You can't berate yourself into positive change! Self-compassion actually goes a lot further. For moments when you're being extra hard on yourself, this exercise will help you lighten up.

WHAT TO DO

It's time to reroute your self-critical thoughts toward a more compassionate and empowering vision. Beside each car on the following page, write a self-critical thought you've had about a current situation. Inside the car, write a self-empowering statement, one that's going to drive you forward! For example, maybe your self-critical thought is "I never do anything right; look what happened at work today." Reroute that to "I do lots of things right, actually; this is just a bump in the road and a learning opportunity!"

Plan Your Daily Nonnegotiables for Self-Care

Self-care is a key component of building self-confidence and curbing those pesky self-doubts. When you take good care of yourself, you're saying "I'm worth the effort." This is why you're going to plan out your daily self-care nonnegotiables, the daily things you refuse to skip when it comes to taking care of *you*.

WHAT TO DO

Fill out the time log with your daily nonnegotiables for taking care of yourself. Examples might include practicing good sleep hygiene, showering, brushing your teeth, and exercise. Commit to always making time for these practices: You deserve this care.

TIME	SELF-CARE NONNEGOTIABLE

Take a Self-Compassion Break

Self-compassion is very important for making your self-doubt less powerful and allowing your self-love to reign. So you're going to take a break right here, right now, for self-compassion!

WHAT TO DO

Bring a situation to mind that is causing you self-doubt. Let yourself feel the stress throughout your body. Then follow these steps:

1. *Acknowledge the pain (e.g., "This may feel uncomfortable but it's worth it.").*

2. *Remember your humanity (e.g., "This doubt is part of being human.").*

3. *Take a deep breath and repeat a few self-compassionate statements (e.g., "I can get through this.").*

4. *Take three more deep breaths and then slowly open your eyes to end the practice.*

APPENDIX

Self-confidence is a journey, not a destination, which is why continuing to consume uplifting and positive content that makes you feel empowered is crucial for building that self-esteem muscle and banishing self-doubt. The following is a list of helpful resources to help you do just that!

Headspace

Headspace is a one-stop mental health app that provides mindfulness tools, mental health coaching, guided meditations, and more. Learn more at Headspace.com.

HelpGuide.org

An independent nonprofit, HelpGuide.org is a clearinghouse for many respected mental health publications, providing valuable education, tools, resources, and advice for living well.

National Alliance on Mental Illness (NAMI)

NAMI is a US-based grassroots organization that provides support, education, and advocacy for people with mental illness and their families. You can find them at NAMI.org.

PositivePsychology.com

This online community's website is a great place to find positive psychology resources, including activities for building self-esteem.

Psychology Today Therapist Directory

The website for the Psychology Today magazine (PsychologyToday.com) includes a tool that can match you with a therapist based on your location, health insurance, and other concerns.

The Mighty

An online community and app centered around mental health and wellness. Find a range of personal stories at TheMighty.com.

Verywell Mind

A platform for information on a range of mental health topics, with articles written by and vetted by professional practitioners. Explore the offerings at VerywellMind.com.

ABOUT THE AUTHOR

Molly Burford writes about relationships, emotional intelligence, and authentic living. Her writing has appeared in *Allure*, *Teen Vogue*, and *Thought Catalog*, among others. She is the author of *The No Worries Workbook*, *Say Yes to Yourself*, *DIY Bucket List*, and *Stop Overthinking*. Molly was born and raised, and still resides, in Detroit, Michigan. Follow Molly at @MollyBurford and learn more at MollyBurford.com.